A SYLLABUS OF THE
HISTORY OF WESTERN EUROPE

BY

FRANKLIN CHARLES PALM, Ph.D.

GINN AND COMPANY
BOSTON · NEW YORK · CHICAGO · LONDON
ATLANTA · DALLAS · COLUMBUS · SAN FRANCISCO

21597

march 1946

The Athenæum Press

GINN AND COMPANY · PRO-
PRIETORS · BOSTON · U.S.A.

PREFACE

During recent years many educators have maintained that our colleges and universities should offer a general course in world history for undergraduates, contending that the present cannot be understood without a knowledge of the whole sweep of the past. Some teachers, however, feel that a course in world history is so broad that a student gets "a little bit of everything, but not much of anything." The writer has attempted to outline a compromise course which will give the student a fair grasp of past events, institutions, and beliefs essential to an understanding of our own age, at the same time placing the greatest emphasis upon the modern period.

This syllabus has been arranged in such a way that the instructor can adjust it to his own needs. If he prefers to cover only the history of western Europe, he can omit assignments II and III (Part One) and devote two weeks each to two of the following assignments: V, VI, X, XV, and XVI (Part Two). Should he desire to omit the "background" material entirely and give a course on the modern period, beginning with the Renaissance, he can leave out assignments II–IX (Part One) and devote two weeks each to eight of the following assignments: XV and XVI (Part One), and I, III, VI, IX, XI, XII, XIII, and XVI (Part Two).

Having these alternatives in mind, the writer has increased the number of references for collateral reading on the modern period, so that the instructor should have no trouble in finding satisfactory material. As a rule the books are arranged in the following order: (1) source collections, (2) general histories, (3) special works. The references, however, are not exhaustive;

they are merely lists of books that the author has used and found suitable for undergraduates. It may well be that a number of changes in the readings and in the map assignments will prove desirable. Nevertheless it is hoped that this syllabus will help to shape the general introductory course in European history so that the student will be able to appreciate the value of history and will be prepared for advanced work.

FRANKLIN CHARLES PALM

BERKELEY, CALIFORNIA

CONTENTS

INTRODUCTORY STATEMENT

This syllabus was originally prepared for use in the introductory European history course in the University of California. In this course the more significant facts, personalities, movements, and institutions are emphasized by means of lectures, readings in a variety of books, geographical exercises, discussions, and frequent written work. A small amount of elementary instruction is also given in modern methods of historical study.

Each of the two parts of the syllabus, covering the work for one semester, is divided into sixteen weekly assignments. The class meets twice a week as a whole for lectures, and once a week for discussion, in sections of about thirty students. The topics treated in each weekly assignment have been outlined in the syllabus. All students are required to read the "principal assignments," and, in addition, to select from the "collateral readings" material to total each week not less than sixty-five pages in the first semester and seventy-five pages in the second.

Once during each semester the student selects a book for rapid collateral reading, out of which a minimum of 250 pages is required. Individual reports on these collateral readings are made by personal conference or in writing. In connection with the book that he chooses in the second semester, each student prepares a short bibliography, making use of the card catalogue in the library, the periodical indexes, and other helps. Students are encouraged to read more than the minimum assignments, especially in the "collateral readings," according to their individual taste. Credit is given for such additional work.

Special attention is given to note-taking. Students are expected to do this, for better comprehension of the subject and to preserve for later years a record of what they have done. The instructors examine the notes at times for the purpose of advising the students. It is recommended that notes on lectures be taken as fully and with as careful organization as possible. Notes on required readings need not be so ample but should represent a careful selection from the material read. Notes on all other readings should be brief, containing a general outline of the subject, and a few remarks about the author and his method of treatment.

Each student should purchase a supply of outline maps and should form the permanent habit of locating geographically every event about which he reads. Copies of most of the books mentioned in the syllabus should be on reserve in the college library, although students may well begin to build up a library by the purchase of the following books:

BREASTED, J. H., *Ancient Times, A History of the Early World.* Boston, 1916.
ROBINSON, J. H., *An Introduction to the History of Western Europe,* 2 vols. Boston, 1926.
SHEPHERD, W. R., *Historical Atlas.* New York, 1921.
PLOETZ, C., *Handbook of Universal History.* New York, 1915.
HASSALL, A., *European History Chronologically Arranged.* London, 1898.

All references are inclusive.

A SYLLABUS OF THE
HISTORY OF WESTERN EUROPE

OUTLINE AND WEEKLY ASSIGNMENTS

PART ONE. THE BACKGROUND OF MODERN HISTORY

I. THE HISTORICAL POINT OF VIEW

A. Purpose and methods of the course.
B. Importance and scope of history.
  1. Definition of history.
  2. Why we should study history.
  3. Its unity or continuity.
  4. Value of a study of western European history.
  5. Kinds of books to be read in a study of western Europe.
     a. Secondary works.
     b. Sources.
  6. The "upshot" of history.

Principal Assignment

  Robinson, *An Introduction to the History of Western Europe*, Vol. I, pp. 1–16.

II. ANCIENT CIVILIZATIONS

A. Division of the early history of mankind into the Age of Stone, the Age of Bronze, and the Age of Iron.

  1. Impossibility of fixing dates for the Stone, the Bronze, and the Iron Age; in some parts of the world these ages overlap each other; continued existence of people in early stages of civilization.
  2. Broca's division: prehistoric man, the man of the Stone Age; protohistoric man, the man of the Metal Ages.
  3. Division of prehistoric man into eolithic, paleolithic, and neolithic man.
    a. The question of eolithic man, or of the existence of man in the tertiary period of the geologist.
    b. Paleolithic man (early and middle Stone Age).
      (1) A hunter,—therefore a nomad and follows the game; later becomes a herdsman.
    c. Neolithic man (late Stone or Bronze and Iron Age).
      (1) Neolithic man lives in villages.
      (2) The age of cultivation begins.
      (3) Early thought.

B. Egyptian civilization.

  1. The geography of Egypt; importance of invention of writing.
  2. Slow development of Egyptian civilization; the Pyramid Age.
  3. Egyptian civilization during the period of the empire.
  4. Egypt after the fall of the empire (1150 B.C.).

C. The civilizations of western Asia.

  1. Babylonia.
    a. The Sumerians; their civilization.
    b. The Semites; desert wanderers.

  c. Conquest of Sumerians by Semites; rise of the great Babylonian civilization (about 2750 B.C.).

2. Rise of the Assyrian Empire.

  a. Organization; culture; decline.

3. The Chaldean Empire.

  a. Reign of Nebuchadnezzar (604–561 B.C.).

   (1) Babylon; its golden age.

   (2) Civilization of Chaldean Empire.

4. The Hebrews.

  a. Rise of the Hebrew kingdom (about 1025–930 B.C.); beginnings of the Bible.

  b. The Babylonian captivity of the Hebrews.

  c. Restoration of the exiled Hebrews by the Persian kings.

  d. Contributions to civilization; the Old Testament.

5. The Persian Empire.

  a. Indo-European; races and languages.

  b. The Medes and the Persians; their religion.

  c. Conquest of Cyrus.

  d. The Persian Empire under Darius the Great (521–485 B.C.).

6. Our debt to Egypt and western Asia.

Principal Assignment

  BREASTED, *Ancient Times, A History of the Early World*, pp. 1–34; ROBINSON, SMITH, and BREASTED, *Our World Today and Yesterday*, pp. 5–26.

Map Study

  (Map of Mediterranean world.) Locate the important empires and cities of ancient times.

Collateral Reading

  Select so that, together with the principal assignment, at least sixty-five pages are read each week.

  BOTSFORD, *A Source Book of Ancient History*, pp. 1–65.

  BREASTED, *Ancient Times*, selections from Part II, The Orient.

III. EARLY DEVELOPMENT OF EUROPEAN CIVILIZATION; GREECE

A. Rise of Greek civilization.
  1. Inventions and knowledge of the east spread to the west.
  2. The predecessors of the Greeks; the Ægeans.
  3. The Cretan civilization.
  4. The Greeks destroy the Ægean civilization.
  5. Development of Greek culture.
      a. Phœnicians carriers of eastern civilization to the west.
      b. The Homeric civilization.
      c. Economic and social development in Greece.
      d. Political evolution.
B. Rise of the Athenian Empire.
  1. Defeat of the Persians.
  2. Rivalry between Athens and Sparta.
      a. Political developments; Athens under Pericles.
      b. Peloponnesian wars (459–404 B.C.).
      c. The hegemony of Sparta.
  3. Contributions of Greek civilization.
      a. Education.
      b. Architecture.
      c. Sculpture.
      d. Literature.
      e. Philosophy.
  4. Expansion of Greek civilization.
      a. Empire of Alexander the Great.
      b. The civilization of the Hellenistic Age.
          (1) Alexandrian civilization.

Principal Assignment

ROBINSON, SMITH, and BREASTED, *Our World Today and Yesterday*, pp. 27–57.

Map Study

(Outline map of the Mediterranean world.) Locate the empire of Alexander the Great, and its important cities.

Collateral Reading

BOTSFORD, *A Source Book of Ancient History*, pp. 67–109, 123–150, 180–209, 283–310.

BREASTED, *Ancient Times*, Parts III and IV, selections.

KNIGHT, *Economic History of Europe to the End of the Middle Ages*, chap. i.

IV. ROMAN CIVILIZATION; WESTERN EUROPE BEFORE AND AFTER THE BARBARIAN INVASIONS

A. Origin of Rome and the establishment of the Roman Republic.
  1. Its government.
B. Expansion of Rome.
  1. Conquest of Carthage.
  2. Conquest of the east.
C. Transition from a republic to an empire.
  1. Reasons for change,—political, social, and economic.
  2. Rise of one-man power.
D. Extent and strength of the Roman Empire.
  1. The age of Augustus (30 B.C.–A.D. 14).
  2. Civilization of the Roman Empire.
    a. Buildings.
    b. Roads.
    c. Literature.
    d. Christianity.
  3. Boundaries and peoples.
  4. The five great bonds of union.
E. Reasons for the decline of the Roman Empire.
  1. Taxation.
  2. Slavery.
  3. Deterioration of land.
  4. Infiltration of barbarians.
F. Culture and religion of the later Roman Empire and the rise of the Christian church.
  1. Rome's borrowed civilization.
  2. Religion.
    a. Importance in Greece and Rome.
    b. The rise of the Christian church.

3. Division of the Roman Empire into eastern and western halves.

  a. Constantinople; her place in history.

G. Fall of the Roman Empire.

  1. The German invasions.

    a. The Goths and the Huns.

    b. "What happened in 476."

    c. Theodoric the Ostrogoth and his conquest of Italy (493).

    d. Emperor Justinian (527–565) and his attempt to oppose the barbarians.

      (1) The Justinian code.

H. Rise of the Frankish kingdom.

  1. The Merovingians.

I. The "upshot" of the Barbarian invasions.

  1. Romans and barbarians mingle, probably because of the small number of the latter.

  2. The Romance languages develop.

  3. Christianity remains.

  4. Both Roman and German law prevail.

  5. Science, art, literature, and education decline but do not wholly perish.

Principal Assignment

ROBINSON, SMITH, and BREASTED, *Our World Today and Yesterday,* pp. 58–82, and ROBINSON, *An Introduction to the History of Western Europe,* Vol. I, pp. 17–55.

Map Study

(Europe.) Locate the principal rivers, mountain ranges, seas, bays, and gulfs of Europe. Also trace the boundary of the Roman empire before its fall, and the movements of the barbarian tribes when they entered the empire.

(As a fixed rule, all places mentioned in the principal assignment are to be located as a part of the map study of the week.)

Collateral Reading

ROBINSON, *Readings in European History*, Vol. I, pp. 14–33.

BOTSFORD, *A Source Book of Ancient History*, pp. 371–378, 397–415, 521–557.

OGG, *A Source Book of Medieval History*, pp. 32–67, 196–202.

MUNRO and SELLERY, *Medieval Civilization*, pp. 18–49, 60–86.

BREASTED, *Ancient Times*, pp. 553–572, 607–617, 636–664.

ADAMS, *Civilization during the Middle Ages*, pp. 65–76, 89–106.

EMERTON, *An Introduction to the Study of the Middle Ages*, pp. 22–59, 62–91.

DILL, *Roman Society in the Last Century of the Western Empire*, pp. 245–281, 285–345.

KNIGHT, *Economic History of Europe*, chap. ii.

V. CHRISTIANITY, MOHAMMEDANISM, AND THE FRANKISH EMPIRE

A. The strength of the medieval church.
1. Adapts itself to the ideas and needs of the time.
2. Emphasizes life after death.
3. Claims to be the one agent of salvation.
4. Assumes temporal as well as spiritual power in preserving law and order after the fall of the Roman Empire.
B. Origin and growth of the papacy.
1. The theory of Petrine supremacy.
2. The Roman church as a mother church of the west.
3. The church fathers and the position of the bishop of Rome.
4. The growth of the church under Leo the Great (440–461) and Gregory the Great (590–604).
   a. Leo's assertion of the supremacy of the Roman bishop.
   b. How Gregory the Great strengthens the spiritual and establishes the temporal power of the pope.
C. Monasticism.
1. Reasons for monasticism.
2. Life of a monk in medieval times.
3. Importance of the monks as missionaries.
   a. The conversion of England and of the Germans.
D. The rise and spread of Mohammedanism.
1. Mohammed, the prophet (570–632).
2. The Mohammedan religion as portrayed in the Koran.
3. The rise of Mohammedan civilization.
E. The Frankish empire.
1. Charles Martel lays the foundation.
2. Pippin the Short becomes king by elective and by divine right (751).

3. The pope obtains the "States of the Church" from Pippin; significance of this act.
4. Charlemagne's place in history.
    a. As a man.
    b. As an organizer and creator of governmental institutions.
    c. As a promoter of culture and enlightenment.
5. Reasons for disruption of Charlemagne's empire (814–887).
    a. Numerous partitions of the empire after his death.
    b. Lack of ability and power to control great states on the part of his successors.
    c. Empire too large.
        (1) Poor means of communication.
        (2) Lack of money to pay officials and army.
    d. New invasions from all sides.
6. Reasons for the existence of the state after the break-up of Charlemagne's empire.
    a. The respect for the king as a ruler by divine right and head of a nation.
    b. Feudalism holds the landowners together and substitutes a feudal state for a national state.

Principal Assignment

ROBINSON, *An Introduction to the History of Western Europe*, Vol. I, pp. 56–123.

Map Study

Be prepared to show, on an outline map, the regions inhabited by Mohammedans and the territories controlled by Charlemagne in 800.

Collateral Reading

ROBINSON, *Readings*, Vol. I, pp. 62–82, 114–124.
MUNRO and SELLERY, *Medieval Civilization*, pp. 114–136.
ADAMS, *Civilization during the Middle Ages*, pp. 107–169.
DUNN PATTISON, *Leading Figures in European History*, Charlemagne.
EMERTON, *Introduction to the Middle Ages*, pp. 93–134; 151–213.
MUNRO, *The Middle Ages*, chaps. ix–xi, xix.

VI. FEUDALISM AND THE EMERGENCE OF THE MODERN NATIONAL STATE

A. Feudalism.
  1. Conditions in ninth and tenth centuries; absence of strong central authority; independence of landed proprietor; earlier Roman and German customs.
  2. The three essentials of feudalism:
     a. The fief (economic side).
     b. Vassalage (social side).
     c. Immunity (political side).
  3. The nobility; qualifications, privileges, ranks, and duties.
B. The emergence of the modern national state.
  1. Rise of the French monarchy.
     a. The early Capetian rulers; problems and achievements.
  2. Rise of England.
     a. England's place in history.
     b. Anglo-Saxon England. The age of invasions.
        (1) Danish invasions and Alfred the Great (871–901).
        (2) Danish conquest of England.
        (3) The Norman invasion and the subjugation of England.
           (*a*) William the Conqueror and the importance of his conquest of England.
           (*b*) General significance of the Norman conquest.
     c. Early Plantagenet England (1154–1307).
        (1) The reforms of Henry II in government and in law.
        (2) Quarrel between Henry II and Archbishop Becket over church courts and jurisdiction.

(3) Struggle between the Plantagenet kings of England and Philip Augustus of France over English possessions in Europe.

3. Early development of absolutism in France.

  a. Philip Augustus, Louis VIII, and Louis IX (St. Louis, 1180–1270) prepare the way for the modern French monarchy.

  b. Philip the Fair (1285–1314) establishes absolutism.

4. Early development of constitutionalism in England.

  a. King John (1199–1216) grants the Magna Carta,—the so-called Great Charter of English liberties; its significance.

  b. Development of Parliament during the reign of Henry III and Edward I (1216–1307).

  (1) Reasons for opposition to king.

  (2) The calling of the Parliaments of 1265 and 1295.

  (3) The inauguration of Parliamentary government; importance.

  c. The conquest of Wales and Scotland.

5. The Hundred Years' War; first of the great European struggles.

  a. Causes of strife.

  b. The conflict to the Treaty of Bretigny (1360).

  c. Outbreak of the war after Bretigny.

  (1) Effects of the war upon France and England.

  (2) French patriotism as manifested in the career of Joan of Arc.

  (3) Reasons for the decline of English domination in France.

  (4) Results of the Hundred Years' War.

    (*a*) Strengthens power of absolute king in France.

    (*b*) Enables English people to concentrate upon domestic instead of European affairs, and later to create a great empire.

Principal Assignment

ROBINSON, *An Introduction to the History of Western Europe*, Vol. I,
pp. 124–178.

Map Study

(Europe.) Locate the lands claimed by the king of England during the
Hundred Years' War. Also designate the important places associated with the conflict.

Collateral Reading

ROBINSON, *Readings*, Vol. I, pp. 171–241, 466–475.
MUNRO and SELLERY, *Medieval Civilization*, pp. 159–167, 168–187,
224–239.
OGG, *Source Book*, pp. 203–232.
ADAMS, *Civilization during the Middle Ages*, pp. 194–226, 311–356.
MUNRO, *The Middle Ages*, chaps. xii, xvi–xviii, xxii.
SEIGNOBOS, *The Feudal Régime*, chap. ii, The Nobles and the Higher
Clergy.
ADAMS, *The Growth of the French Nation*, pp. 54–72, 108–135.
CHEYNEY, *A Short History of England*, pp. 102–262.
GREEN, *A Short History of the English People*, pp. 44–104.
MORRIS, *The Early English County Court*, pp. 89–121, 131–146.
MORRIS, *The Medieval English Sheriff*, pp. 115–124.

VII. THE CONFLICT BETWEEN THE SPIRITUAL AND TEMPORAL EMPIRES IN THE MIDDLE AGES

A. The papal-imperial struggle.
  1. Origin of the Holy Roman Empire.
     a. Growth of *Stem duchies*; lack of national unity.
     b. Increase of royal power in Germany.
        (1) Reasons for a confederation under a king.
        (2) Early German kings.
     c. The revival of imperial authority by the coronation of Otto I by the pope (962).
        (1) Significance of that event.
  2. Condition of the church in the eleventh century.
     a. Decline in strength and dignity because of its great wealth.
        (1) The church drawn into the feudal system.
     b. Emphasis of church upon spiritual prerogatives of the clergy.
     c. Emphasis of king upon secular power of the clergy.
     d. Complicated situation confronting the bishops.
     e. The questions of investiture, celibacy of the clergy, and simony.
     f. Demoralized condition of papacy.
     g. Church reform.
  3. The papal-imperial struggle (1073–1122).
     a. Claims of papacy as announced by Pope Gregory VII.
     b. His plan of reform.
     c. Struggle between Gregory and Henry IV over lay investiture; Canossa.
     d. A compromise: the Concordat of Worms (1122).
  4. The conflict between the papacy and the Hohenstaufens.

    a. Frederick I (1152–1189).

       (1) Forces opposed to imperialism: vassals, popes, Lombard cities.

    b. The rise of the Lombard towns.

    c. The conflict between towns and emperor.

       (1) The peace at Constance (1183).

    d. Henry VI (1190–1197), and his attempt to make Italy a part of the Holy Roman Empire.

    e. Pope Innocent III as arbiter of Europe.

       (1) His part in the German situation.

       (2) His intervention in England.

    f. The conflict between Frederick II and the papacy.

    g. Decentralization in Germany and in Italy.

B. The Crusades.

    1. Causes: persecutions of pilgrims; appeal from Emperor Alexis; crusading councils; privileges for crusaders.

    2. The First Crusade; the great militant monastic orders.

    3. The Second, Third, and Fourth Crusades.

    4. Results: commercial, intellectual.

Principal Assignment

    ROBINSON, *An Introduction to the History of Western Europe*, Vol. I, pp. 179–225.

Map Study

    (Map of the Near East.) Trace the routes of the first four crusades.

Collateral Reading

    ROBINSON, *Readings*, Vol. I, pp. 245–260, 266–293, 296–306, 329–342.

    MUNRO and SELLERY, *Medieval Civilization*, pp. 137–152, 188–209, 212–223, 248–268.

    DUNN PATTISON, *Leading Figures*, Hildebrand (Pope Gregory VII) and Frederick II.

    ADAMS, *Civilization during the Middle Ages*, pp. 227–278.

    HENDERSON, *A Short History of Germany*, Vol. I, pp. 49–101.

    MUNRO, *The Middle Ages*, chaps. xxi, xxv, The Crusades.

    EMERTON, *Medieval Europe*, pp. 240–356.

VIII. THE MEDIEVAL CHURCH AT ITS HEIGHT

A. Medieval and modern churches; comparison.
B. The medieval church.
  1. Organization.
     a. The pope, the all-powerful head.
     b. The bishop; the parish.
  2. The seven sacraments; significance.
  3. Importance of the clergy.
  4. Corruption among the clergy.
  5. Heretics, the anarchists of the middle ages.
     a. Opposition to them.
        (1) Reform of abuses in the church.
        (2) Use of military force.
        (3) The Inquisition.
        (4) Religious orders.
  6. The rise of religious orders.
     a. The Franciscans; the Dominicans.
  7. The question of church and state in the fourteenth century.
     a. Boniface VIII and Philip the Fair.
     b. The Babylonian captivity of the church (1305–1377).

Principal Assignment

ROBINSON, *An Introduction to the History of Western Europe*, Vol. I, pp. 226–259.

Collateral Reading

MUNRO and SELLERY, *Medieval Civilization*, pp. 153–158, 432–457.
EMERTON, *Medieval Europe*, pp. 541–592.
MUNRO, *The Middle Ages*, chap. xiii.
JESSOPP, *The Coming of the Friars*, pp. 1–52.
SABATIER, *Life of St. Francis of Assisi*, pp. 53–87.
Catholic Encyclopedia, article on Boniface VIII.

IX. MEDIEVAL LIFE AND CULTURE

A. The people in country and town.
  1. The country: the manor or villa; the serfs; system of agriculture; monotony and misery of country life; gradual breakdown of manorial system.
  2. The towns; origin and appearance of medieval towns; industry and gilds; commerce and its obstacles.
    a. Hanseatic League.
B. The culture of the middle ages.
  1. Languages and literature.
    a. Troubadours and chivalry.
    b. Science.
  2. The fine arts: painting, sculpture, and architecture.
    a. Cathedrals.
  3. Universities of the middle ages.
  4. Learning of the middle ages.
    a. Scholasticism.
  5. Contrast between the early and later middle ages.

Principal Assignment

  ROBINSON, *An Introduction to the History of Western Europe*, Vol. I, pp. 260–309.

Map Study

  (Map of world.) Show principal medieval trade routes to the Levant and to the Far East.

Collateral Reading

  ROBINSON, *Readings*, Vol. I, pp. 399–412, 415–428, 431–461.
  OGG, *Source Book*, pp. 339–359.
  MUNRO and SELLERY, *Medieval Civilization*, pp. 240–247, 310–347, 348–357, 358–365, 458–473, 474–484.

ADAMS, *Civilization in Medieval Europe*, pp. 279–310.
CHEYNEY, *A Short History of England*, pp. 36–57, 59–83.
EMERTON, *Medieval Europe*, pp. 26–28, 471–476, 509–540.
JESSOPP, *The Coming of the Friars*, pp. 53–112, 262–301.
THORNDIKE, *The History of Medieval Europe*, pp. 373–432.
HENDERSON, *Short History of Germany*, Vol. I, pp. 111–121.
HASKINS, *The Rise of Universities*, pp. 79–126.
KNIGHT, *Economic History of Europe*, chaps. iii–vi.

X. THE RENAISSANCE; ITS SIGNIFICANCE

A. The Renaissance.
  1. Definitions.
    a. A "new birth" of learning.
    b. A change in thought and taste, in books, buildings, and pictures.
    c. A new attitude toward life.
  2. Origins.
    a. Crusades; spirit of industry and commerce; increasing wealth; the Italian cities and city life; presence of classical antiquity and of Greek scholars.
  3. Influence of the Renaissance.
    a. Literature and scholarship.
      (1) Dante, Petrarch, Boccaccio, Chrysoloras.
      (2) Humanism; the study of the classics.
      (3) The invention of printing.
B. Fine arts.
  1. Architecture and sculpture: Niccola of Pisa, Ghiberti, Michelangelo.
  2. Painting: Giotto, Fra Angelico, Leonardo da Vinci, Michelangelo, Raphael.
C. Explorations and discoveries.
  1. Need of a new route to Spice Islands.
  2. Curiosity and the spirit of adventure.
  3. The explorers and discoveries: Vasco da Gama, Columbus.
D. Renaissance science: Copernicus.
E. Individualism: Cellini.

Principal Assignment
  ROBINSON, *An Introduction to the History of Western Europe*, Vol. I, pp. 310–340.

Map Study

(Italy.) Study the subdivisions of Italy in the fifteenth century. Which among the chief towns were noted for devotion to art? learning? religion? trade? political rule?

Collateral Reading

ROBINSON, *Readings*, Vol. I, pp. 516–541.

OGG, *Source Book*, pp. 444–473.

WHITCOMB, *A Literary Source Book of the Renaissance*, pp. 1–7, 84–90.

DUNN PATTISON, *Leading Figures*, Lorenzo de' Medici.

ADAMS, *Civilization during the Middle Ages*, pp. 364–391, The Renaissance.

THORNDIKE, *The History of Medieval Europe*, pp. 576–612.

EMERTON, *The Beginnings of Modern Europe*, pp. 461–533.

ROBINSON and ROLFE, *Petrarch*, pp. 227–294.

REINACH, *Apollo*, chaps. xv–xviii.

Cambridge Modern History, Vol. I, chap. xvi, The Classical Renaissance.

SYMONDS, *A Short History of the Renaissance in Italy*, pp. 1–51, 121–131, 149–186, 197–240.

XI. EUROPE AT THE OPENING OF THE SIXTEENTH CENTURY

A. Political history; its purpose.
B. Wars of the Roses and the rise of Tudor despotism.
  1. Weakening of the power of the nobles.
C. Evidences of the drift toward absolutism in France.
  1. The creation of the standing army.
  2. Taxes collected by the king.
  3. Limitation of power of nobles.
  4. The achievements of Louis XI.
D. The Holy Roman Empire under Charles V.
  1. The rise of the house of Hapsburg.
    a. Weak position of the emperor.
    b. Election of Rudolph of Hapsburg.
  2. Unification and expansion of Spain.
  3. The marriage alliance resulting in the union of the Spanish and Holy Roman Empires under Charles V.
E. Italy, the debatable ground of the sixteenth century.
  1. French invasions.
F. The beginning of the struggle for the balance of power in the sixteenth century.

Principal Assignment

ROBINSON, *An Introduction to the History of Western Europe*, Vol. I, pp. 341–364.

Map Study

(Europe.) Locate the territories of Charles V; the territories of England; the territories of France before Charles's abdication (1556).

Collateral Reading

ROBINSON, *Readings*, Vol. II, pp. 1–27.

THORNDIKE, *The History of Medieval Europe*, pp. 614–639.

ADAMS, *The Growth of the French Nation*, pp. 136–159.

GRANT, *The French Monarchy (1483–1789)*, Vol. I, pp. 1–16.

SEEBOHM, *The Era of the Protestant Revolution*, pp. 1–68.

JOHNSON, *Europe in the Sixteenth Century*, pp. 1–128.

CHEYNEY, *European Background of American History (1300–1600)*, pp. 60–122.

Encyclopædia Britannica, article on Charles V (emperor).

XII. THE BACKGROUND OF THE PROTESTANT REVOLT

A. The Protestant revolt, of political and social as well as religious significance.
B. The state of ecclesiastical affairs prior to the Reformation.
　1. Early criticism of the church.
　　a. Pierre Dubois.
　　b. Marsiglio of Padua.
　　c. Wycliffe.
　2. The Babylonian captivity (1305–1377).
　3. The Great Schism (1378–1417).
　　a. The Council of Constance (1414–1418).
　　　(1) Problems and achievements: healing of schism; extirpation of heresy; reformation of church.
　　b. The Council of Ferrara-Florence (1438–1442).
　　　(1) Pope the head of the church.
　　　(2) Development of interest in Greek literature in Italy.
　4. The Renaissance popes.
C. Reason for origin of the religious revolt in Germany.
　1. Lack of unity and limited authority of emperor.
　2. Power in hands of ambitious vassals.
　3. Social and economic conditions in Germany.
　　a. Towns, centers of culture and wealth.
　　b. Growing middle class; luxury and ease.
　　c. Decline of knights; their hatred for middle class.
　　d. Oppression of peasants; their hatred for nobles.
　4. Political conditions.
　　a. Bewildering subdivisions of Germany.
　　b. No real central power to settle local, political, territorial, or religious disputes.

5. Religious enthusiasm in Germany before the revolt.
6. Political, social, and religious reformers in the sixteenth century.
    a. Erasmus, humanist and citizen of the world.
    b. Sir Thomas More; his *Utopia*.
7. The agitation in Germany against the papal curia.
    a. The minnesinger, Walter von der Vogelweide.
    b. Ulrich von Hutten.

Principal Assignment

ROBINSON, *An Introduction to the History of Western Europe*, Vol. I, pp. 365–402.

Collateral Reading

ROBINSON, *Readings*, Vol. II, pp. 31–50.
SEEBOHM, *The Era of the Protestant Revolution*, pp. 68–97.
SMITH, *The Age of the Reformation*, pp. 3–61.
SMITH, *Erasmus*, pp. 1–58.
HENDERSON, *A Short History of Germany*, Vol. I, pp. 228–250.
SCHAPIRO, *Social Reform and the Reformation*, chaps. i, ii.

XIII. GERMANY AND THE PROTESTANT REVOLT

A. The beginning of the Protestant revolt.
1. Luther's career to 1517; justification by faith.
2. Abuses with regard to indulgences; the ninety-five theses (1517).
3. The disputation with Eck at Leipzig (1519).
4. Luther's friends and enemies.
5. Luther's appeal to the country.
   a. The three tracts (1520).
      (1) Liberty of the Christian man.
      (2) Address to the German nobility.
      (3) The Babylonian captivity of the church.
6. Luther's break with the old order.
   a. The Diet of Worms (1521).
7. Luther at the Wartburg; his policy of moderation.
   a. Translation of the Bible; significance.
8. The violent revolution begins.
   a. Certain princes use the religious issue to increase their power.
   b. The church attempts to avoid the break by adopting moderate reforms at Ratisbon.
   c. The peasants revolt to obtain social justice (1524–1525).
9. Development of the revolt.
   a. The first and second diet of Speyer (1526, 1529).
      (1) The prince obtains control over religion.
   b. The Augsburg Confession.
   c. The Schmalkaldic League (1531) and civil war (1547–1552).

    d. The Peace of Augsburg.
        (1) Freedom of conscience and control of religion by
            rulers.
        (2) Toleration for Catholics and Lutherans only.

Principal Assignment

ROBINSON, *An Introduction to the History of Western Europe*, Vol. I,
pp. 403–435.

Map Study

(Europe.) Be able to locate places associated with the career of
Luther.

Collateral Reading

ROBINSON, *Readings*, Vol. II, pp. 53–117.
DUNN PATTISON, *Leading Figures*, Martin Luther.
SCHEVILL, *A History of Europe*, pp. 91–119.
SCHAPIRO, *Social Reform and the Reformation*, chaps. iii, iv.
SEEBOHM, *The Era of the Protestant Revolution*, pp. 97–171.
WALKER, *Great Men of the Christian Church*, Martin Luther.
VEDDER, *The Reformation in Germany*, pp. 3–108.
SMITH, *The Age of the Reformation*, pp. 62–145.
Catholic Encyclopedia, and Schaff-Herzog, *The New Encyclopedia of
Religious Knowledge*, articles on Luther.
Cambridge Modern History, Vol. II, chap. iv, Luther.

XIV. CALVINISM AND THE SPREAD OF PROTESTANTISM

A. Protestantism in Switzerland.
1. The Zwinglian revolt from Rome.
    a. Swiss political conditions.
    b. Zwingli's break with Rome (1523).
    c. Religious and civil wars in Switzerland.
    d. Importance of Zwingli's revolt.
2. Calvin's revolt from the church.
    a. His early life.
    b. The "Institutes of the Christian Religion" (1536).
    c. Calvin at Geneva (1536).
        (1) His plan for a Puritan commonwealth.
        (2) His doctrine of predestination.
    d. Spread of Calvinism; its significance.
        (1) Presbyterianism; the so-called *Westminster Confession of Faith.*
        (2) Spread in France, Germany, Holland, England, Scotland, and America.
B. Protestantism in England.
1. England's revolt from the church.
    a. Early opposition to Rome; the enlightened ideas of Cardinal Wolsey.
    b. Protestantism and the divorce case of Henry VIII.
    c. The revolt of the English church from Rome (1534).
    d. Significance of the revolt.
        (1) Government controls the church.
        (2) Henry VIII plunders the monasteries.
        (3) Theology not changed.

2. Introduction of Protestantism into England.
   a. Attempts to establish Protestantism after death of Henry VIII (1547).
      (1) Cranmer and the prayer book (1549).
      (2) The Thirty-nine Articles and the Act of Uniformity (1552).
   b. Catholic reaction.
      (1) Mary ascends the throne of England.
      (2) Her religious policy.
3. Parliamentary opposition to Mary.
   a. The revolt, and her marriage to Philip II of Spain.
   b. Religious persecution during Mary's reign.
   c. Religious situation in England at the time of her death (1558).

Principal Assignment

ROBINSON, *An Introduction to the History of Western Europe*, Vol. I, pp. 435–458.

Map Study

(Europe.) Be able to locate places associated with the careers of Zwingli and Calvin.

Collateral Reading

ROBINSON, *Readings*, Vol. II, pp. 118–152.
SCHEVILL, *A History of Europe*, pp. 121–134.
JACKSON, *Huldreich Zwingli*, Introductory chapter and chap. xvi.
SEEBOHM, *The Era of Protestant Revolution*, pp. 171–198.
WALKER, *Great Men of the Christian Church*, John Calvin.
Catholic Encyclopedia and Schaff-Herzog, *The New Encyclopedia of Religious Knowledge*, articles on Calvin and Zwingli.

XV. POLITICAL AND RELIGIOUS WARS

A. The Catholic Reformation.
   1. Early attempts to alter the organization and teachings of the church.
   2. The Council of Trent.
      a. Upholds the sacraments and the Vulgate.
      b. Advocates reforms of the clergy.
      c. Establishes a new and solid foundation for law and doctrine of the Catholic church.
      d. Establishes the Index of prohibited books.
   3. The Society of Jesus.
      a. Ignatius Loyola, the founder.
      b. Organization and object of the Society.
      c. Achievements of the Jesuits.
      d. History of the organization.
   4. The great secular leader of the church, Philip II.
      a. Predominance of Spain in the sixteenth century.
      b. Religious policy of Charles V.
      c. Philip's religious policy.
   5. The revolt of the Netherlands.
      a. Reasons for revolt.
         (1) Dislike of Philip II.
         (2) Political and religious grievances.
         (3) Taxes. + Customs -
      b. William, prince of Orange.
         (1) The revolt; the meeting of the representatives of the Netherlands at Ghent (1576).
      c. The northern provinces refuse to recognize Philip as king; the Union of Utrecht.

    d. Later history of the revolt.
      (1) Queen Elizabeth's policy.
      (2) The defeat of the Armada (1588).
      (3) Independence of Dutch (United Provinces) fully
          recognized (1648).
    e. Significance of Dutch success.
      (1) Political and economic development of the Dutch
          empire.

B. The so-called religious wars in France.
  1. Spread of Protestantism in France.
  2. Governmental opposition to the Huguenots.
  3. The boy kings and Catherine de' Medici.
  4. Political and religious motives pave the way for civil wars.
    a. The eve of St. Bartholomew's Day (August 23, 1572).
    b. The Politiques; Henry of Montmorency-Damville.
  5. The three Henrys and the rise of Navarre to the throne.
  6. Henry IV saves the French monarchy.
    a. Religious toleration granted by Edict of Nantes (1598).
    b. Sully and the economic development of France.
    c. The way is paved for the rise of the great French ab-
        solute monarchy of the seventeenth century.

C. England's golden age.
  1. Elizabeth's wise reign.
    a. Peace in England.
    b. Economic development.
    c. Social life.
    d. The age of great writers.
  2. The religious question during the reign of Elizabeth.
    a. Elizabeth's conservative policy and her attempt to
      maintain peace.
      (1) She establishes the church of England (Anglican
          church).
  3. Elizabeth and Mary Stuart.
    a. Presbyterianism in Scotland.

b. The Scotch queen, Mary Stuart.

    (1) Her career.

    (2) Her abdication in favor of her infant son James VI and her appeal to Elizabeth.

c. Plots against Elizabeth.

    (1) Relations between Philip II of Spain and Elizabeth.

    (2) The Irish question and Elizabeth.

    (3) The Jesuits in England.

    (4) Mary's execution.

4. Philip II's attempt to intervene in English affairs.

    a. The "Invincible Armada."

5. The religious situation in Europe before and after the death of Philip II.

6. The last phase of the religious wars,—Thirty Years' War.

    a. Causes.

        (1) Unsolved religious problems.

        (2) Lack of unity in Holy Roman Empire.

        (3) Catholic Counter-Reformation.

    b. The Bohemian and Palatine period (1618–1623).

        (1) The "Winter King."

    c. The Danish period (1625–1629).

        (1) Wallenstein.

    d. The Swedish period (1630–1635).

        (1) Gustavus Adolphus and Swedish ambitions.

    e. The French period (1635–1648).

        (1) Richelieu.

            (*a*) The decline of the Hapsburgs.

            (*b*) The rise of absolutism and mercantilism in France.

    f. The Treaties of Westphalia (1648).

        (1) Religious settlements and territorial adjustments.

        (2) Effects of the war upon Germany.

        (3) The rise of the Hohenzollerns.

7. General results of the religious wars.

Principal Assignment

ROBINSON, *An Introduction to the History of Western Europe*, Vol. I, pp. 459–497.

Map Study

(Europe.) Show the European possessions of Philip II. Also outline the boundaries of Bohemia, Brandenburg, and the Duchy of Prussia after 1648. Indicate the territorial gains of Brandenburg-Prussia and Sweden by the Treaty of Westphalia.

Collateral Reading

ROBINSON, *Readings*, Vol. II, pp. 156–216.

DUNN PATTISON, *Leading Figures*, Philip II and Gustavus Adolphus.

CHEYNEY, *A Short History of England*, pp. 330–381.

SMITH, *The Age of the Reformation*, pp. 609–624, 641–651.

SEEBOHM, *The Era of the Protestant Revolution*, pp. 218–238, General Results of the Period.

VAN DYKE, *Ignatius Loyola*, pp. 151–191.

WALKER, *Great Men of the Christian Church*, Ignatius Loyola.

PALM, *Politics and Religion in Sixteenth Century France*, chaps. i–iii, vii–x.

PALM, "Mercantilism as a Factor in Richelieu's Economic Policy," *Political Science Quarterly*, Vol. XXXIX, pp. 650 ff.

HENDERSON, *A Short History of Germany*, Vol. I, pp. 456–497.

CHAPMAN, *A History of Spain*, pp. 303–323.

WAKEMAN, *Europe, 1598–1715*, pp. 14–38, 132–153.

Encyclopædia Britannica or *Catholic Encyclopedia*, articles on Council of Trent (see under Trent, Council of), Loyola (see Ignatius in *Catholic Encyclopedia*), Philip II, and Elizabeth (in *Encyclopædia Britannica* only).

XVI. THE RISE OF CONSTITUTIONALISM IN ENGLAND AND THE CULMINATION OF ABSOLUTISM IN FRANCE

A. England.
1. James I,—ambition to be an absolute ruler (1603–1625).
   a. His theories of government.
   b. His relations with
      (1) Parliament.
      (2) Other countries.
   c. Intellectual development in spite of James I.
2. Charles I attempts to become an absolute ruler (1625–1649).
   a. His wars.
   b. His quarrels with Parliament.
   c. The celebrated Petition of Right.
   d. Religious complications.
   e. Quarrels over religion and taxes.
3. The religious controversy.
   a. Archbishop Laud tries to make all the people Anglicans.
   b. The low-church party, or *Puritans*, refuse to conform, and the Presbyterians agree with them.
   c. The Separatists, or Independents, reject both the Anglican and the Presbyterian organizations.
      (1) The "Pilgrim Fathers" cross the sea.
4. Charles I tries to make the Scotch Presbyterians conform.
   a. Calls Parliament to his aid.
5. The Long Parliament instead executes Charles I (1649).
   a. Oliver Cromwell, leader of the *Roundheads*.
   b. The Westminster Assembly.

6. The Commonwealth, or republic.
   a. Cromwell's conquest of Ireland and Scotland.
   b. Cromwell attacks the Dutch,—England's commercial rival.
      (1) The Navigation Act (1651).
   c. Cromwell quarrels with Parliament and makes himself Lord Protector of England.
      (1) His successful foreign policy.
7. The Restoration.
   a. Charles II (1660–1685) enjoys the kingship.
   b. His Parliament attacks the Presbyterians and the Independents.
   c. Charles advocates religious toleration.
   d. His relations with Louis XIV.
8. The "Glorious Revolution" of 1688.
   a. James II attempts to reëstablish the Catholic church.
   b. The accession of William and Mary (1689).
      (1) The Bill of Rights; its importance.
      (2) The Toleration Act.
   c. General significance of the revolution.
B. France.
   1. Achievements of Richelieu and Mazarin.
   2. Louis XIV becomes an absolute ruler.
      a. Louis XIV has interesting ideas about the kingship.
         (1) His two great advantages over James I.
      b. The golden age of France.
         (1) Versailles.
         (2) Economic development under Colbert.
         (3) Art, literature, and science.
      c. Louis XIV's attempts to overturn the "Balance of Power."
         (1) Important motives behind his wars.
            (*a*) To enhance his prestige in France.
            (*b*) To gain the "natural limits" of France.

(2) The wars of Louis XIV.
    (*a*) War of the Spanish Netherlands (1667–1668).
    (*b*) The war against the Dutch (1672–1678).
    (*c*) War of the Palatinate (1689–1697).
    (*d*) War of the Spanish Succession (1701–1713).
(3) The revocation of the Edict of Nantes (1685); its significance.
(4) The Treaties of Utrecht and Rastadt (1713–1714); importance.
(5) France at the close of Louis's reign.
    (*a*) A demoralized kingdom.
    (*b*) Absolutism on the decline.

Principal Assignment

ROBINSON, *An Introduction to the History of Western Europe*, Vol. I, pp. 498–531.

Map Study

(Europe.) Show the territories gained by Louis XIV in the first three wars, and also the partition of the European possessions of Spain in 1713–1714.

Collateral Reading

ROBINSON, *Readings*, Vol. II, pp. 218–297.
DUNN PATTISON, *Leading Figures*, Louis XIV.
WHITE, *Seven Great Statesmen*, Grotius.
SCHEVILL, *A History of Europe*, pp. 314–328.
CHEYNEY, *A Short History of England*, pp. 383–464.
SEELEY, *Expansion of England*, Lecture II, England in the Eighteenth Century.
BRIDGES, *France under Richelieu and Colbert*, Lecture III, pp. 82–124.
TREVELYAN, *England under the Stuarts*, pp. 73–99.
WAKEMAN, *European History, 1598–1715*, pp. 184–205.
VOLTAIRE, *Age of Louis XIV*, Vol. II, chaps. xxv–xxviii, Anecdotes of Louis XIV.

Rapid Collateral Reading.

The student should read during the semester a minimum of 250 pages from one of the books listed below, and should be prepared to give an individual report either in personal conference or in writing.

SAYCE, *Babylonians and Assyrians, Life and Customs.*

MAHAFFY, *Social Life in Greece from Homer to Menander.*

DAVIS, *The Influence of Wealth in Imperial Rome.*

DAVIS, *Charlemagne.*

LUCHAIRE, *Social France at the Time of Philip Augustus.*

HASKINS, *The Normans in European History.*

JESSOPP, *The Coming of the Friars.*

SABATIER, *Life of St. Francis of Assisi.*

LANE-POOLE, *Saladin.*

LANE-POOLE, *The Story of the Moors.*

DAVIS, *Life on a Medieval Barony, a Picture of a Typical Feudal Community in the Thirteenth Century.*

McCABE, *Peter Abélard.*

PATER, *The Renaissance.*

SICHEL, *The Renaissance.*

ARMSTRONG, *Lorenzo de' Medici and Florence in the Fifteenth Century.*

RICHMAN, *The Spanish Conquerors.*

BOLTON, *The Spanish Borderlands.*

WOOD, *Elizabethan Sea-Dogs.*

MUNRO, *Crusaders of New France.*

ALLEN, *The Age of Erasmus.*

SMITH, *Erasmus, a Study of his Life.*

VAN DYKE, *Ignatius Loyola.*

JACOBS, *Martin Luther.*

LYBYER, *The Government of the Ottoman Empire in the Time of Suleiman the Magnificent.*

HUME, *Philip II of Spain.*

PUTNAM, *William the Silent.*

PALM, *Politics and Religion in Sixteenth Century France.*

MORLEY, *Oliver Cromwell.*

BEESLEY, *Queen Elizabeth.*

PERKINS, *Richelieu.*

HUGON, *Social France in the XVII Century.*

FARMER, *Versailles and the Court under Louis XIV.*

HASSALL, *Louis XIV.*

PART TWO. MODERN EUROPEAN HISTORY

I. THE DRAWING TOGETHER OF EASTERN AND WESTERN EUROPE

A. Importance of eastern European history.
  1. Tendency of western European history to merge into world history.
  2. The Near East as a factor in recent European history.
  3. Contributions of the east to present-day civilization.
B. Early history of the east.
  1. Nomadic invasions.
  2. The Slavs in the Balkans.
    a. Early invasions.
    b. The three branches of Slavs.
    c. Origin of Bulgaria.
      (1) The Bulgars.
      (2) Bulgaria's golden age under Boris (852–884) and Simeon I (893–927).
      (3) Bulgaria in decline.
  3. The rise of the Hungarian state.
    a. The Hungarian, or Magyar, race.
      (1) Arrival of Magyars in Hungary (895).
    b. Hungary's golden age under Stephen I (997–1038).
      (1) The Slavs in Hungary.
  4. Russia in the early days.
    a. The Slavs in Russia.
    b. Invasion of the Northmen; Rurik (862).
    c. Vladimir the Great (980–1015): struggle with Poland.

5. Serbia and Bulgaria in the time of the Crusades.
   a. Bulgaria.
   b. Conquest by the Turks.
6. The break between the Latin and Greek churches.
   a. Reasons for break; the *schismatic* church.
      (1) Cyril's alphabet and Slav unity.
7. Early attacks upon Constantinople.
   a. By western Christians during Crusades.
   b. By Mongols.
      (1) Jenghiz Khan and Kublai Khan.
      (2) The Polo brothers visit China; influence of China on western history.
   c. Invasion of Turks.
      (1) Origin of Turks; adoption of Mohammedanism.
      (2) Capture of Constantinople (1453).
8. Golden age of Turkey in reign of Suleiman the Magnificent (1520–1566).
   a. Expansion of Turkish empire.
   b. Siege of Vienna (1683) and decline of Turkish empire.
9. Growth of Russia before Peter the Great.
   a. Consolidation of territory around the princes of Moscow.
   b. Early development of Russian autocracy.
      (1) The Romanov dynasty (1613).
10. Peter the Great and his efforts to Europeanize Russia.
    a. Early life; policies and significance of his reign.
11. Rise of Prussia.
    a. Northern Germany in the middle ages; the North Mark; Brandenburg and Prussia.
    b. Rise of the house of Hohenzollern.
    c. The Great Elector (1640–1688); his policies and achievements.
    d. Frederick III, elector of Brandenburg; "King in Prussia."
    e. Frederick William I; "the barrack king."

Principal Assignment

ROBINSON, *An Introduction to the History of Western Europe*, Vol. II, pp. 1–43.

Map Study

(World.) Locate the empire of Jenghiz Khan and of Suleiman the Magnificent. Also indicate the lands acquired by Peter the Great and Frederick William, the Great Elector. Be prepared to locate the important rivers, mountains, and cities in seventeenth-century Russia.

Collateral Reading

(During this semester a total of 75 pages, including the text, should be read each week.)

ROBINSON, *Readings*, Vol. II, pp. 301–319.

MORFILL, *Russia*, chaps. i–vii.

GIBBON, *The History of the Decline and Fall of the Roman Empire*, Vol. V, chaps. liii–lvi; Vol. VI, chaps. lxiv–lxvi.

HENDERSON, *A Short History of Germany*, Vol. II, chaps. i–iii.

MORFILL, *Poland*, chaps. vii–x.

MILLER, *The Balkans*, Part II, chap. ii; Part III, chap. ii.

BAIN, *The First Romanovs*, pp. 340–367.

BEAZLEY and others, *Russia from the Varangians to the Bolsheviks*, Book II, chaps. iv, v.

LANE-POOLE, *Turkey*, chaps. i, vii, x, xi.

MARRIOTT and ROBERTSON, *The Evolution of Prussia*, pp. 37–111.

LYBYER, *The Government of the Ottoman Empire in the Time of Suleiman the Magnificent*, selections.

WAKEMAN, *European History, 1598–1715*, chaps. viii, xiii.

PARES, *A History of Russia*, chaps. xi, xii.

Encyclopædia Britannica, articles on John Sobieski (see John III of Poland), Charles XII (of Sweden), and Peter (the Great of Russia).

II. DYNASTIC WARS AND EUROPEAN EXPANSION IN THE EIGHTEENTH CENTURY

A. Importance of military and diplomatic history.
B. Dynastic wars in the eighteenth century.
  1. War of the Spanish Succession and the Great Northern War; significance.
  2. War of the Polish Succession (1733–1735).
    a. Austrian and Spanish ambitions in Italy.
    b. The significance of the Polish war.
      (1) To Spain and Austria in Italy.
      (2) To France in Lorraine.
  3. Italy, the Holy Roman Empire, and Russia in the eighteenth century.
C. The rise of Prussia under Frederick the Great.
  1. Frederick's youth; wide range of interests.
  2. Maria Theresa and the Pragmatic Sanction.
    a. The war of the Austrian Succession (1740–1748).
      (1) Significance.
    b. Peace of Aix-la-Chapelle (1748).
  3. The Seven Years' War (1756–1763).
    a. Important nations and rulers involved.
    b. The diplomatic revolution.
    c. Frederick as a military leader.
    d. Peace of Paris (1763); significance.
D. The spread of absolutism resulting in the partitions of Poland, 1772, 1793, and 1795.
  1. Circumstances leading to the partitions of Poland.
  2. The standards of international morality of the eighteenth century.

E. Decline of France and rise of the British Empire.

1. The diffusion of western-European civilization among all mankind; European expansion in the eighteenth century.

    a. Results of that expansion.

2. The rise of the British Empire.

    a. India, the jewel.

        (1) Its geography, peoples, and history.

            (*a*) Invasion of Tamerlane (1398); the Mogul Empire.

        (2) Its religions.

    b. The British and French struggle for India.

        (1) Early English trading stations in India, and the struggle between the English and Dutch for commercial supremacy.

        (2) Rise of French dominion in the east.

            (*a*) Colbert.

        (3) Struggles between French and English East India companies during first half of eighteenth century; Dupleix and Clive.

    c. Fall of French empire and rise of English power in India.

        (1) Conflicts with natives.

        (2) English graft, corruption, and oppression in India; trial of Warren Hastings (1778).

        (3) Parliamentary control of India.

    d. The French and Indian War in America.

        (1) Relative strength of British and French possessions in the New World (1750).

        (2) The war and its results (Peace of Paris 1763).

    e. The American Revolution.

        (1) Causes.

        (2) The war; French assistance.

        (3) Significance.

Principal Assignment

ROBINSON, *An Introduction to the History of Western Europe*, Vol. II, pp. 44–95.

Map Study

(World.) Can you discern geographical reasons for the respective locations of the colonial possessions of Spain, Portugal, France, Holland, and England? What other things helped to determine the location? Outline the colonial possessions of these countries as they were about 1750.

Collateral Reading

ROBINSON, *Readings*, Vol. II, pp. 319–356.

DUNN PATTISON, *Leading Figures*, Frederick the Great.

LAVISSE, *Youth of Frederick the Great*, chap. iii.

YOUNG, *Frederick the Great*, pp. 359–400.

CARLYLE, *Frederick the Great*, Books I, IV.

HENDERSON, *A Short History of Germany*, Vol. I, chap. iv.

MACAULAY, *Critical and Historical Essays*, Vol. I, Lord Clive, Warren Hastings, and Vol. II, Frederick the Great.

DAY, *A History of Commerce*, chaps. xix–xxi, xxiv–xxvii.

PARKMAN, *Montcalm and Wolfe*, Vol. II, chap. xxvii, The Heights of Abraham.

PRIEST, *Germany Since 1740*, chaps. i–iii.

BOLTON and MARSHALL, *The Colonization of North America (1492–1783)*, selections.

III. NEW INQUIRIES ABOUT OLD BELIEFS IN SEVENTEENTH-CENTURY AND EIGHTEENTH-CENTURY EUROPE

A. Importance of the scientist and philosopher in history.
  1. History of the expansion of human knowledge.
  2. Questioning in the seventeenth century.
     a. Francis Bacon (1561–1626), the herald of scientific research.
     b. The development of modern chemistry, astronomy, and the physical sciences.
        (1) Roger Bacon and his three methods of reaching truth.
        (2) Ancient beliefs in alchemy and astrology.
        (3) Achievements of Lavoisier, Galileo, Newton, and Leeuwenhoek.
     c. Founding of scientific journals, academies, and expeditions.
  3. The great scientific discovery of the early modern period; belief in natural and immutable laws.
  4. Misunderstandings between scientists and theologians.
     a. Development of the deistic movement; Lord Herbert of Cherbury.
        (1) Tendency to "enlarge God" and revise the traditional idea of Him.
        (2) Attacks upon ancient beliefs about Satan.
           (*a*) The decline of witchcraft.
  5. Natural law as against the "Divine Right" theory.
     a. Government in theory and government in practice are generally two different things.

    b. Important changes of theories concerning earthly rule in the seventeenth and eighteenth centuries.

        (1) Results of these changes; rise of ideas of sovereignty of the people; separation of church and state; rise of middle class; growth of nationalism; attempts to obtain world peace.

6. Decline of monarchical form of government.

    a. The "Divine Right" idea as set forth by English and French writers; Bossuet.

    b. The events in the seventeenth century which weakened the theory of "Divine Right" and the authority of kings in England.

    c. Diminution of governmental control over public opinion.

        (1) Milton; opposition to censorship of books.

        (2) Locke; opposition to governmental right to interfere with freedom of religion.

7. The importance of Holland as a place for intellectual refugees.

    a. Achievements of Descartes, Spinoza, Le Clerc, and Bayle.

8. Modernism; the moderns question the superiority of the classics.

    a. Montaigne, Wotton, Bentley, and Fontenelle.

9. The great eighteenth-century philosophers and their influence in France.

    a. Voltaire; life; attacks upon church; his beliefs; his place in history.

    b. Diderot and the Encyclopædia; the significance of his work.

    c. Montesquieu and his scientific study of government; "The Spirit of the Laws."

    d. Rousseau; the prophet of democracy.

    e. Beccaria; criminal sociology.

10. The birth of modern political economy and "free trade" (*Laissez-faire*).
    a. Mercantilism.
11. Present-day importance of intellectual developments in seventeenth-century and eighteenth-century Europe.

Principal Assignment

ROBINSON, *An Introduction to the History of Western Europe*, Vol. II, pp. 96–161.

Collateral Reading

ROBINSON and BEARD, *Readings in Modern European History*, Vol. I, pp. 172–199.

MATHEWS, *The French Revolution*, chap. vi.

LOWELL, *The Eve of the French Revolution*, chaps. v, x, xvi, xvii, xviii, and xix.

SCHEVILL, *A History of Europe*, pp. 384–403.

Cambridge Modern History, Vol. VIII, chap. i, Philosophy and the Revolution.

IV. MEDIEVALISM, CONSTITUTIONALISM, AND PATERNALISM IN THE EIGHTEENTH CENTURY

A. Origin of the modern idea of general progress.
  1. Condorcet's ideas.
B. Rural and city life in the eighteenth century.
  1. The peasant; gradual extinction of serfdom.
  2. The towns; the guild system.
C. The privileged class; the decline of the nobility.
D. Church and state.
  1. Traditional ideas of church.
  2. Four great issues between church and state.
  3. Attempts to limit power of pope.
  4. Ultramontanism and Gallicanism.
    a. The Jesuits, defenders of papal power.
  5. The church in the eighteenth century.
  6. Lack of toleration.
E. Religious situation in England.
  1. The "dissenters"; Quakers and "Methodists."
  2. Act of Toleration (1689).
F. Origin of constitutional government in England.
  1. Parliament as compared with the Estates General.
  2. The question of suffrage in England.
  3. Political parties; Tories and Whigs.
  4. Rise of cabinet government.
  5. Politics in eighteenth-century England.
G. Paternalism in the eighteenth century; the enlightened despots.
  1. Frederick the Great, Catherine II, Joseph II, and Charles III of Spain.

Principal Assignment

ROBINSON, *An Introduction to the History of Western Europe*, Vol. II, pp. 162–194.

Map Study

(Europe.) Hand in an outline showing boundaries of principal states of Europe in 1789.

Collateral Reading

MATHEWS, *The French Revolution*, chaps. i–v.

LOWELL, *The Eve of the French Revolution*, chaps. i–iv, vi–ix, xi–xv.

PERKINS, *France under Louis XV*, Vol. I, chap. i ; Vol. II, chap. xxiii.

BOURNE, *The Revolutionary Period in Europe*, pp. 48–61, The Work of the Enlightened Despots.

ADAMS, *Outline Sketch of English Constitutional History*, chap. ix, The Making of the Cabinet.

YOUNG, A., *Travels in France by Arthur Young*, selections.

SÉE, *Economic and Social Conditions in France during the Eighteenth Century*, selections.

Encyclopædia Britannica, articles on Joseph II (emperor) and Charles III (King of Spain).

V. THE FRENCH REVOLUTION AND THE PASSING OF THE *OLD RÉGIME*

A. Importance of the French Revolution.

 1. The key to an understanding of Europe today.

B. Causes of the Revolution.

 1. Political situation when Louis XVI became king.

 2. Laws, customs, duties, and taxes.

 3. Unpopularity of the privileged classes; the clergy and the nobility.

 4. The third estate; the peasant.

 5. French despotism; king and *parlements*.

    a. Opposition of the philosophers and economists.

C. Reign of Louis XVI.

 1. His marriage to Marie Antoinette.

 2. The king tries to become a benevolent despot.

    a. Turgot; attempt to save France from bankruptcy.

    b. Necker; report on the financial condition of France.

    c. Calonne; borrow and spend freely.

 3. The calling of the Estates General (1789).

    a. The assembly of "Notables" (1787).

      (1) Influence of the *parlement* of Paris.

    b. Estates General becomes a constitutional assembly.

      (1) Vote "by order" or "as individuals."

      (2) "The Tennis-Court Oath" (June 20, 1789).

        (*a*) Count Mirabeau.

 4. The rise of the Paris mobs.

    a. Destruction of the Bastille (July 14, 1789).

    b. Creation of the "national guard" and of the Paris *commune*.

5. Reforms of the national assembly; passing of the *old régime*.

    a. The "great fear."

    b. Celebrated night session of August 4–5.

    c. Reform of local administration.

    d. "Declaration of the rights of man and of the citizen"; importance.

6. The National Assembly (October, 1789–September, 1791).

    a. The march to Versailles (October 5).

    b. Hatred between *bourgeoisie* and Paris mob; Marat.

    c. Constitution of 1791; provisions; defects.

    d. Secularization of church property; *assignats.*

    e. Civil Constitution of the Clergy (July, 1790).

        (1) Catholic opposition to the Revolution.

7. Importance of work of National Assembly.

8. Opposition to National Assembly.

    a. The government and foreign rulers.

    b. The populace in Paris.

Principal Assignment

ROBINSON, *An Introduction to the History of Western Europe,* Vol. II, pp. 195–236.

Collateral Reading

ROBINSON, *Readings,* Vol. II, pp. 386–427.

MATHEWS, *The French Revolution,* chaps. ix–xiv.

HAZEN, *Modern Europe,* pp. 66–116.

WHITE, *Seven Great Statesmen,* Turgot.

CARLYLE, *The French Revolution,* Part I, Book IV, chap. iv.

STEPHENS, *French Revolution,* Vol. I, pp. 291–309, 340–367.

FLING, *Source Problems on the French Revolution,* Problem IV.

Encyclopædia Britannica, articles on Mirabeau and the French Revolution.

VI. FROM A REPUBLIC TO A DICTATORSHIP

A. The Legislative Assembly (1791–1792).
  1. The *émigrés.*
  2. The flight to Varennes (June, 1791).
  3. "A republican party demands democracy."
  4. The "Massacre of the Champs de Mars."
  5. Foreign hostility to the French Revolution.
  6. Influence of newspapers.
  7. Rise of political clubs; Jacobins, Girondists.
  8. Acts of legislative assembly against *émigrés* and clergy.
  9. Precipitation of war between France and Austria (April 20, 1792); significance.
  10. The manifesto of the duke of Brunswick (July, 1792).
      a. Attack on the Tuileries (August 10, 1792).
      b. A new *revolutionary commune* is formed, and the king is suspended.
      c. France declared a republic by the new convention, September 22, 1792 (Year I of French liberty).
B. The National Convention (1792–1795).
  1. The *commune* of Paris institutes the reign of terror.
  2. Republican army defeats Austrians.
  3. Convention proposes to use its armies to revolutionize Europe.
  4. Trial and execution of king (January 21, 1793).
  5. The first coalition against France.
      a. Its aims.
  6. The reign of terror.
      a. Origin.
      b. Struggle between Girondist and Mountain parties.

    c. The Vendean royalists, and revolts against the Convention in Marseille, Bordeaux, and Lyon.

    d. Carnot, the "organizer of victory."

7. Terror the order of the day.

    a. Governmental machinery used to crush internal and external enemies.

    b. Execution of Marie Antoinette and Madame Roland.

    c. Opposition to terror.

    d. Hébert and the worship of Reason.

    e. Robespierre and Saint-Just.

        (1) Importance; the Great Terror.

        (2) The reaction.

8. Importance and nature of the reign of terror.

    a. Reforms of the National Convention.

9. The Constitution of Year III; the Directory.

    a. The attack upon the Convention.

    b. Its defender—Napoleon Bonaparte.

C. The rise of Napoleon Bonaparte.

  1. His youth.

  2. His Italian campaign (1796–1797).

  3. His character and ambitions.

  4. The Egyptian campaign (1798).

  5. The *coup d'état* (November 9, 1799).

  6. Napoleon as First Consul.

  7. Napoleon's ability as an administrator.

  8. The second campaign against Austria (1800–1801).

    a. Peace of Amiens (1802).

    b. Spain's cession of Louisiana to France.

  9. Bonaparte and the consolidation of Germany; its significance.

Principal Assignment

    ROBINSON, *An Introduction to the History of Western Europe*, Vol. II, pp. 237–283.

Map Study

(Europe.) Trace Napoleon's campaigns, note the principal changes in national boundaries, and observe the rearrangement of Germany by Napoleon.

Collateral Reading

MATHEWS, *The French Revolution*, chaps. xv–xxi.
HAZEN, *Modern Europe*, pp. 118–185.
JOHNSTON, *Napoleon*, pp. 1–70.
FISHER, *Napoleon*, pp. 7–56.
BOURNE, *The Revolutionary Period in Europe*, pp. 169–231.
MADELIN, *French Revolution*, chaps. xxxix–xlix.
FOURNIER, *Napoleon the First*, chaps. iv, vi.
WRIGHT, *The Background of Modern French Literature*, pp. 20–36.
BOURRIENNE, *Memoirs of Napoleon Bonaparte*, Vol. I, chaps. ix–xi.
MORLEY, *Critical Miscellanies*, Vol. I, Robespierre.
CARLYLE, *The French Revolution*, Part III, Book IV, chap. iv.
Encyclopædia Britannica, articles on Robespierre and Danton.

VII. THE NAPOLEONIC EMPIRE AND ITS DOWNFALL

A. Napoleon as a statesman.

B. General Bonaparte as emperor of the French (December 2, 1804).

C. Napoleon as a general; war with Austria (the Third Coalition, 1805).

    1. Reasons for the formation of the Coalition.

    2. Prussia's policy.

    3. Campaign against Austria; Ulm, Austerlitz.

    4. Treaty of Pressburg (1805).

        a. End of the Holy Roman Empire (1806).

    5. Trafalgar (1805).

D. The humiliation of Prussia; Jena (1806).

E. Treaty of Tilsit (1807); the alliance of the two emperors.

F. Napoleon's desperate attempt to defeat England; the Continental Blockade.

    1. English declaration of 1806.

    2. The Berlin and Milan decrees.

    3. The United States and the Blockade.

    4. Part played by Continental Blockade in bringing about downfall of Napoleon.

G. Napoleon at the zenith of his power.

    1. His administration.

    2. His despotism.

    3. Napoleon's attempt to control Spain.

        a. The national uprising.

        b. English intervention.

    4. War with Austria (1809).

5. The Campaign against Russia (1812).
6. Josephine and Maria Louisa.
7. The Napoleonic empire at its height.

H. Fall of the Napoleonic empire.

1. Growing spirit of nationalism.
2. Failure to conquer England, Russia, and Spain.
3. The regeneration of Prussia.
    a. Educational and moral reform.
    b. Development of nationalism.
    c. Military reorganization.
4. The Fall of Napoleon.
    a. The War of Liberation; Leipzig (1813).
    b. Elba: the Hundred Days; Waterloo (1815); Saint Helena.

Principal Assignment

ROBINSON, *An Introduction to the History of Western Europe*, Vol. II, pp. 284–316.

Map Study

(Europe.) Be able to trace the military movements of Napoleon and to locate his battles and the political states which he set up. Study also the geographical details of his treaties.

Collateral Reading

ROBINSON, *Readings*, Vol. II, pp. 490–529.
HAZEN, *Modern Europe*, pp. 186–232.
DUNN PATTISON, *Leading Figures*, Napoleon.
JOHNSTON, *Napoleon*, pp. 118–187.
GUÉRARD, *French Civilization in the Nineteenth Century*, pp. 55–85.
ROSE, *The Life of Napoleon I*, Vol. II, pp. 146–159, 449–471.
FOURNIER, *Napoleon the First*, chaps. xii, xiii.
BOURNE, *The Revolutionary Period in Europe*, pp. 340–366, 400–413.
MAHAN, *Influence of Sea Power upon the French Revolution and Empire*, Vol. II, pp. 331–357.
Encyclopædia Britannica, article on Napoleon I.

Rapid Collateral Reading

Prepare a bibliography of not less than ten items based on the title of the book in which you are doing your rapid collateral reading. Use the card catalogue and the periodical indexes in the library. Write each reference in good form on a separate card 4 × 6 inches in size. Characterize each reference in about twenty words.

A typical card reduced in size:

LIBRARY NUMBER	ROBINSON, JAMES HARVEY
	An Introduction to the History of Western Europe, 2 vols., Boston, 1926.
	A clear, well-written, and comprehensive textbook of European history from the fall of the Roman Empire to 1926. Provided with carefully selected maps and an excellent list of books for additional reading.

VIII. THE AGE OF CONSERVATION (1815-1848)

A. The Congress of Vienna (1814–1815).
1. Significance.
2. Treatment of France after Napoleon's fall.
3. Settlements arranged at the Congress of Vienna.
4. The controversy over the disposition of Polish territory; importance of settlement.
5. The principle of "legitimacy."

B. Suppression of liberalism.
1. Metternich; Holy Alliance and Quadruple Alliance.

C. Solution of the German problem at the Congress of Vienna.
1. Chief effects of the Napoleonic occupation of Germany.
2. Various plans for German unity.
3. The confederation of the "Sovereign Princes and Free Towns of Germany."

D. Political and economic movements in Germany.
1. Liberalism and its suppression; Wartburg Festival (1817); Karlsbad Decrees (1819).
2. Constitutional and economic development in Germany.
   a. The *Zollverein* and German economic union.

E. Spain and the revolt of her colonies.
1. Reaction in Spain after fall of Napoleon.
2. Revolt of Spanish colonies in South America.
3. Intervention of France (Congress of Verona, 1822).
4. Significance of the famous Monroe Doctrine (1823).

F. Italy after the fall of Napoleon; "a geographical expression."
1. Napoleon's reforms in Italy; desire for unity.
2. Liberalism in Italy; Carbonari; Neapolitan insurrection (1820).
3. Mazzini and "young Italy."

G. The Restoration in France.
   1. Administration of Louis XVII (1814–1824).
   a. The *Charter* (constitution).
   b. The ultra-royalist party and its attempts to restore the *old régime.*
   2. Administration of Charles X (1824–1830).
   a. Attitude toward liberalism.
   b. Reactionary laws and measures lead to his overthrow.
   3. The revolution of 1830; *bourgeoisie* control government.
   4. Administration of Louis Philippe; the "July Monarchy" (1830–1848).
   a. Reactionary policy of Louis Philippe and Guizot.
   b. Opposition of liberals, republicans, and socialists.
   5. Revolution of 1848 and the establishment of the Second Empire (1852).
H. Belgium and Greece; struggles for independence.

Principal Assignment

ROBINSON, *An Introduction to the History of Western Europe,* Vol. II, pp. 317–340.

Map Study

ROBINSON, *An Introduction to the History of Western Europe,* Vol. II, pp. 317–340.

Collateral Reading

ROBINSON, *Readings,* Vol. II, pp. 533–558.
FLICK, *Modern World History, 1776–1926,* pp. 129–143.
HAZEN, *Europe since 1815,* Vol. I, pp. 1–52, 71–165.
WHITE, *Seven Great Statesmen,* Stein.
SCHEVILL, *History of Europe,* pp. 467–496.
ANDREWS, *The Historical Development of Modern Europe,* Vol. I, chaps. iii, iv.
GUÉRARD, *French Civilization in the Nineteenth Century,* pp. 89–120.
FUETER, *World History, 1815–1920,* pp. 25–100.
WRIGHT, *The Background of Modern French Literature,* chaps. v, viii.
Encyclopædia Britannica, article on Metternich.

IX. REVOLUTION, NATIONALISM, AND DEMOCRACY IN EUROPE, 1848-1914

A. Revolutions of 1848.
1. In Austria, Bohemia, and Hungary; fall of Metternich.
2. In Italy; Charles Albert.
3. In Germany; the National Assembly at Frankfurt.
B. Failure of the revolutions.
1. In Italy; abdication of Charles Albert.
2. In Bohemia; rivalry between Germans and Czechs.
3. In Hungary; rivalry between the Magyars and Slavs.
   a. Kossuth.
   b. The dual federation of Austria-Hungary (1866).
C. Failure to bring about the unification of Germany.
1. Rivalry between Austria and Prussia.
2. Frederick William IV refuses the imperial title.
3. The Prussian constitution.
4. General aims of the revolution of 1848.
D. Unification of Italy.
1. Cavour.
   a. Rise of Piedmont.
   b. Crimean War (1854–1856).
   c. Napoleon III and Piedmont attack Austria (1859).
   d. Plebiscites in central Italy.
   e. Garibaldi and the conquest of southern Italy.
   f. The kingdom of Italy proclaimed (1861).
E. The founding of the North German Federation (1866).
1. Administration of William I of Prussia.
   a. The reorganization of the Prussian army (1862).
   b. Bismarck makes possible the North German Federation.
      (1) He solves the "army problem."
      (2) The Schleswig-Holstein affair (1864).

(3) Bismarck isolates and defeats Austria (1866).

(4) The North German Federation.

F. The Franco-Prussian War (1870–1871).

   1. Causes and preliminaries.

     a. Napoleon III and German unification.

     b. Failure of negotiations for French compensation.

     c. Spanish candidacy of Leopold of Hohenzollern.

     d. The Ems telegram; Bismarck's aims.

   2. The war; Sedan (1870).

   3. The treaty of peace; significance.

   4. Proclamation of the German Empire (January 18, 1871), and the rise of the Third French Republic.

G. The Italian constitutional monarchy.

   1. Italy and the war of 1866 between Prussia and Austria.

   2. The Roman question; Garibaldi in Sicily and Naples; the acquisition of Rome.

   3. Problems confronting modern Italy.

     a. The "Prisoner of the Vatican."

     b. Militarism and imperialism.

     c. Taxation and finance.

     d. Intellectual and economic conditions.

     e. Political problems.

H. The German Empire.

   1. The German government; organization and powers.

   2. The *Kulturkampf* (1872–1879).

   3. Rise of the Social Democratic Labor Party.

     a. Bismarck's attempt to suppress socialism by force.

     b. His effort to conquer socialism with kindness; state socialism.

   4. William II (1888–1918) takes the place of the "iron chancellor," Bismarck.

   5. Germany's economic progress; industry, agriculture, commerce, and colonization.

   6. Germany in 1914,—a world power.

I. The Third French Republic.
1. The government.
2. Paris, the money center of Europe.
3. Education.
4. The relations between church and state.
5. Nationalism and imperialism in France.

Principal Assignment

ROBINSON, *An Introduction to the History of Western Europe*, Vol. II, pp. 341–367.

Map Study

(Central Europe.) Distinguish clearly the areas of the Holy Roman Empire (before 1806), the German Confederation, Austria, Prussia, the North German Federation, and the German Empire. Did these areas conform to nationality or natural boundaries?

Collateral Reading

ROBINSON, *Readings*, Vol. II, pp. 564–596.

FLICK, *Modern World History, 1776–1926*, pp. 231–237, on nationalism; 252–261, on rise of the German Empire; 262–265, on rise of the Dual Monarchy; 301–338, on Third French Republic, the German Empire, and Austria-Hungary before 1914.

HAYES, *A Political and Social History of Modern Europe*, Vol. II, chaps. xxiii, xxiv.

DUNN PATTISON, *Leading Figures*, Cavour and Bismarck.

THAYER, *Throne-Makers*, Bismarck, Kossuth, and Garibaldi.

ROSE, *Development of European Nations*, Part I, pp. 153–183.

GUÉRARD, *French Civilization in the Nineteenth Century*, pp. 150–183.

HENDERSON, *A Short History of Germany*, Vol. II, chaps. viii, x.

DAWSON, *The Evolution of Modern Germany*, chaps. v, xv, xvi, xvii, xix, xx.

PRIEST, *Germany since 1740*, pp. 124–184.

HOWE, *Socialized Germany*, pp. 24–94.

FUETER, *World History, 1815–1920*, pp. 248–314.

OGG, *Social Progress in Continental Europe*, pp. 246–263.

WRIGHT, *The Background of Modern French Literature*, chaps. xii, xiii, xv, xvi.

HANOTAUX, *Contemporary France*, Vol. I, pp. 158–228.

X. THE INDUSTRIAL REVOLUTION; GREAT BRITAIN AND HER EMPIRE

A. Significance of the mechanical revolution.
    1. Hargreaves, Arkwright, Cartwright, Whitney, and Watt.
B. The Industrial Revolution.
    1. Rise of the factory system.
        a. *Capitalist* and *worker.*
        b. Effects upon women and children.
        c. Effects upon European politics and theories of government and industry.
            (1) *Laissez-faire* idea.
            (2) Development of unions.
            (3) Socialism.
C. Influence of Industrial Revolution upon England.
    1. Rise of great industrial centers.
    2. Need for political and social reforms.
D. The English government.
    1. Parliament; the prime minister; the cabinet.
E. Suffrage reforms.
F. Other reforms in England.
    1. The Emancipation Act.
    2. Legal reforms; the public-school system.
    3. Repeal of the so-called Corn Laws.
    4. Social legislation; tax reform.
G. The Irish question.
    1. Irish grievances against England.
    2. Act of Union (1801).
    3. Catholic Emancipation Act (1829).
    4. Gladstone and the land question.
    5. Rise of secret societies in Ireland; Irish nationalists.

6. Home-rule movement.
7. Growth of republican party in Ireland (Sinn Fein).
8. The Irish Free State.

H. The British Empire.
1. Three categories of colonies.
2. Canada.
   a. Lord Durham's report of 1840.
   b. Creation of Dominion of Canada (1867).
3. Australia, Tasmania, and New Zealand.
   a. Creation of Commonwealth of Australia (1900).
   b. Social reform in New Zealand.
4. South Africa; Union of South Africa.
   a. Cape Colony; the Boers; their settlements.
   b. Discovery of gold in Transvaal region (1885).
   c. Boer opposition to extension of British interests in their territory (1899).
   d. The establishment of the Union of South Africa (1910).
   e. Part played by Boers in World War.
5. Other British possessions in Africa.
   a. The proposed Cape-to-Cairo railroad.
   b. English territorial gains in Africa as a result of the World War.
6. British India.
   a. Unique position of India in the British Empire.
      (1) The East India Company.
      (2) Expansion of British power.
   b. Native revolts (1857).
   c. Queen Victoria, empress of India (1877).
   d. Economic development of India.
   e. Gandhi and the nationalist movement.
      (1) The Government of India Act (1919).

Principal Assignment

Robinson, *An Introduction to the History of Western Europe*, Vol. II, pp. 368–395.

Map Study

(Map of world.) Outline the colonial possessions of Great Britain in 1914 and locate the important economic resources found in them.

Collateral Reading

ROBINSON and BEARD, *Readings in Modern European History*, Vol. II, pp. 45–72, 239–337.

FLICK, *Modern World History, 1776–1926*, pp. 155–176, 455–468.

HAYES, *A Political and Social History of Modern Europe*, Vol. II, chaps. xviii, xxii, xxix.

CHEYNEY, *A Short History of England*, pp. 617–678.

FUETER, *World History, 1815–1920*, pp. 7–21.

GIBBINS, *Industrial History of England*, pp. 144–239.

DAY, *A History of Commerce*, chaps. xxviii–xxxviii.

ROBINSON, *The Development of the British Empire*, pp. 131–145, 428–447.

OGG, *Economic Development of Modern Europe*, pp. 133–155.

MOON, *Imperialism and World Politics*, pp. 160–187.

XI. MODERN IMPERIALISM

A. The new industrial revolution.
1. Business on a large scale.
2. Improvements in transportation and communication.
3. Increase of steel output.
4. Suez and Panama canals.
5. Development of telegraph system; the radio.
B. Causes of the colonial revival which brought on the new imperialism.
1. Economic.
a. Export of goods.
b. Export of capital.
c. Colonies sources of raw material.
d. Missionaries as apostles of western ideas.
e. Nationalism and imperialism.
C. Europe and the Far East.
1. Early relations between Europe and China.
a. The Portuguese in China (1557).
b. The opium war (1840–1842).
c. France and England attack China (1856–1860).
2. Early relations between Europe and Japan.
a. Commodore Perry (1853).
b. Europeanization of Japan.
c. War between China and Japan (1894–1895).
D. Development of European imperialism in the Far East.
1. Russia obtains Port Arthur.
2. Germany seizes Kiaochow Bay (1897).
3. England leases Weihaiwei.
4. Alliance between England and Japan (1902).

E. Expansion of western influences in China.
  1. The attempt to westernize the orientals.
    a. Boxer uprising (1900).
    b. The indemnity,—the beginning of the exploitation of China.
    c. The reform movement in China.
  2. Russo-Japanese War blasts Russia's hopes in the Far East (1905).
  3. Creation of a republic in China (1912).
    a. Yuan Shih-k'ai, the dictator.
    b. Dr. Sun Yat-sen sets up an independent government in southern China.
    c. Recent revolutions in China.
      (1) Wu Pei-fu and Tuan Chi-jui.
      (2) The nationalist uprising, Shanghai (1927).
    d. Western exploitation and the attempts of China to adopt western civilization and remain independent.
F. The partition of Africa.
  1. Reason for the "dark continent."
  2. Africa before 1870.
    a. Explorations of Livingstone and Stanley (1840–1878).
  3. Partitions of Africa.
    a. French empire.
    b. German acquisitions in Africa (1884–1890).
    c. Congo Free State (1885).
    d. The English and French struggle for Egypt.
      (1) Mehemet Ali.
      (2) Construction of Suez canal.
      (3) English occupation of Egypt.
      (4) Revolt in the Sudan.
      (5) Economic progress in Egypt.
      (6) Independence of Egypt (1922).
        (*a*) Nationalist demands.
        (*b*) Attitude of England toward nationalism.

G. Hispanic America.
1. End of Spanish dominion in the new world.
2. Rise of the United States as a world power.
3. Hispanic-American states.
4. Pan-Americanism.
5. Political, economic, social, and religious problems in South America and Mexico.
    a. Revolutions in South America.
    b. The question of foreign investments in South America.
    c. Church and state in Mexico; foreign interests there.
    d. The Nicaraguan affair (1927).

Principal Assignment

ROBINSON, *An Introduction to the History of Western Europe,* Vol. II, pp. 396–414.

Map Study

(World.) Note carefully the colonial possessions, as they existed in 1914 (before the war), of France, Germany, Russia, the United States, Italy, Belgium, and Holland. Note territorial changes since 1870.

Collateral Reading

ROBINSON and BEARD, *Readings,* Vol. II, pp. 406–466.
FLICK, *Modern World History, 1776–1926,* pp. 413–454, 469–499.
HAYES, *A Political and Social History of Modern Europe,* Vol. II, chaps. xxvii, xxviii.
VIALLATE, *Economic Imperialism and International Relations during the Last Fifty Years,* pp. 3–91.
GIBBONS, *Introduction to World Politics,* pp. 52–64, 113–129, 166–184.
WOOLF, *Economic Imperialism,* pp. 9–98.
HOBSON, *Imperialism, a Study,* pp. 119–161, 305–346.
FUETER, *World History, 1815–1920,* pp. 317–360.
MOON, *Imperialism and World Politics,* pp. 1–74.
DOUGLAS, *Europe and the Far East,* pp. 144–168, 323–360.
BASSETT, *A Short History of the United States,* pp. 764–781, 809–827.
HARRIS, *Europe and the East,* chaps. xii–xiv.
PRIESTLEY, *The Mexican Nation, a History,* selections.

XII. RUSSIA AND THE NEAR-EASTERN QUESTION

A. Autocratic Russia.
  1. Reasons for Russia's backwardness.
     a. Uninfluenced by the Roman Empire and Roman Catholicism.
     b. Tartar subjection (1240–1480).
     c. Uninfluenced by Renaissance and Protestant revolt.
     d. Lack of ice-free ports. (See assignment in Schapiro, *Modern and Contemporary European History*, in collateral reading, for discussion of above points.)
  2. Reign of Alexander I (1801–1825).
     a. Extent of empire; races and peoples.
     b. Alexander's liberal and reactionary policies.
  3. Reign of Nicholas I (1825–1855).
     a. "Decembrist conspiracy."
     b. His extreme despotism; "frozen Russia."
     c. His foreign policy.
        (1) Suppression of revolt in Hungary.
        (2) Russo-Turkish War (1828–1829).
        (3) Crimean War (1854–1856).
  4. Reign of Alexander II (1855–1881).
     a. Emancipation of serfs.
        (1) Serfdom in Russia.
        (2) The emancipation proclamation (March 3, 1861).
        (3) The *mir* or *village community*.
        (4) Results of emancipation.
     b. Judicial and legal reforms.
     c. Reforms in local government; Zemstvos.

     d. Educational reforms.

     e. Polish rebellion.

     f. Alexander's death; rise of the Russian terrorists.

5. The Revolutionary movement.

     a. The Nihilists; ideas, method of propaganda, terrorism.

     b. Russian novelists; Turgenev, Dostoievsky, Tolstoy.

6. Reign of Alexander III (1881–1894).

     a. His reactionary policy; Russification.

7. Economic expansion of Russia.

     a. Industrial Revolution in Russia.

     b. Railway building; importance.

     c. Sergius J. Witte's successful measures.

     d. Appearance of middle class.

     e. Effects on the revolutionary movement.

8. Reign of Nicholas II (1894–1917).

     a. Training and ideas.

     b. His despotism; Plehve.

     c. Development of opposition to this cruel government.

       (1) The Constitutional Democrats.

       (2) The socialist movement.

         (*a*) Socialist Revolutionary party,—forerunners of the Bolsheviki.

     d. The revolution of 1905; "Red Sunday."

     e. Calling of first *Duma*; what happened.

     f. Abolition of the *mir*; significance.

     g. Nicholas II's oppressive measures lead to the great Revolution (1917). (The assignment in Schapiro, *Modern and Contemporary European History*, in collateral reading, might well be required.)

9. The Near-Eastern question.

     a. Definition.

     b. Russian and Austrian interests in the Near East.

     c. Nationalist movements in the Balkans.

       (1) Serbia obtains independence (1817).

(2) The Greek uprising; international significance.

(3) Greek independence is recognized (1832).

d. The Near East becomes the center of international rivalries.

   (1) The Crimean War (1854–1856) ; causes and results.

   (2) The Russo-Turkish War (1877–1878).

   (a) Insurrections in Bosnia and Herzegovina.

   (b) Attitude of the "great powers."

   1) England's fear of Russia; refuses to act.

   2) Russia's war on Turkey.

   (c) Treaty of San Stefano.

   (d) Congress of Berlin (1878).

   (3) Significance of territorial settlements; Bulgaria.

   (a) Greek war upon Turkey (1897).

   (4) Macedonia, the sore-spot of Europe.

e. The Balkan crisis.

   (1) The Young Turk party.

   (2) The *coup d'état* of 1908.

   (3) The breaking-up of the Turkish Empire.

   (4) The Italian and Turkish War (1911).

   (5) The Balkan Wars (1912–1913).

   (a) The Macedonian question.

   (b) The Balkan alliance.

   (c) First Balkan War; Treaty of London (1913).

   (d) Second Balkan War; Treaty of Bucharest (1913).

   (e) Significance of Balkan Wars. (The assignment in Hayes, *A Political and Social History of Modern Europe*, in the collateral reading below, might well be required.)

Principal Assignment

ROBINSON, *An Introduction to the History of Western Europe*, Vol. II, pp. 415–442.

Map Study

(World and Europe.) Locate the various races in the Russian Empire in 1914 and be prepared to explain why Russian expansion was necessary and inevitable from a geographical point of view. What directions did it take? Also sketch the boundaries of the Balkan states and Turkey in 1914 and show to what extent they conformed to the areas of nationality. What great routes of trade and travel led across the Near East in 1914?

Collateral Reading

ROBINSON and BEARD, *Readings*, Vol. II, pp. 338–405.

SCHAPIRO, *Modern and Contemporary European History*, chaps. xxi–xxiii, xxvii.

HAYES, *A Political and Social History of Modern Europe*, Vol. II, chaps. xxv, xxvi.

FLICK, *Modern World History, 1776–1926*, pp. 267–273, 339–348, 366–410.

HARRIS, *Europe and the East*, chaps. ii, iii.

FUETER, *World History, 1815–1920*, pp. 212–222, 403–422.

ROSE, *The Development of the European Nations*, Vol. I, pp. 344–376.

GOOCH, *History of Modern Europe*, pp. 398–426.

GIBBONS, *The New Map of Europe*, pp. 161–219, 263–350.

GIBBONS, *Introduction to World Politics*, pp. 96–112, 219–227, 246–271.

SCHURMAN, *The Balkan Wars*, pp. 3–60.

MILYOUKOV, *Russia and its Crisis*, selections.

PARES, *A History of Russia*, pp. 449–471.

TOYNBEE and KIRKWOOD, *Turkey*, selections.

Encyclopædia Britannica, articles on Nicholas I (emperor of Russia), The Crimean War, Nicholas II (emperor of Russia), and Turkey.

XIII. THE DIPLOMATIC BACKGROUND OF THE WORLD WAR

A. International relations in early modern history.
  1. "Society of nations" as recognized by the Treaty of Westphalia and in the writings of Grotius.
  2. Significance of American and French Revolutions in international relations.
  3. The "Concert of Europe."
     a. Holy and Quadruple alliances (1815).
     b. Congress of Vienna and the slave trade (1815).
     c. Congress of Paris and neutral trade (1856).
     d. The Geneva Convention (1864).
     e. Activities in the Near East.
        (1) Congress of Vienna (1815).
        (2) Congress of Berlin (1878).
        (3) Balkan Wars (1912–1913).
     f. Conference of Berlin concerning Africa (1884–1885).
     g. Suppression of Boxer uprising (1900).
     h. Algeciras Conference over Morocco (1906).
     i. The two Hague conferences (1899, 1907).
B. The rise of the great system of alliances; the Triple Alliance.
  1. Bismarck's attempts to isolate France after Franco-Prussian War.
  2. The *Dreikaiserbund*, or Three Emperors' League (1872).
  3. The "war scare" of 1875.
  4. Russian and Austrian interests in Near East.
  5. Bismarck checks Russian advance and preserves status quo in Congress of Berlin (1878).
  6. The Dual Alliance between Austria and Germany (1879).

7. The second Three Emperors' League marks victory of Bismarck's policy of preventing war in Near East and isolating France.

8. The formation of the Triple Alliance (1882).
    a. Reasons for Italy's entering into it.
    b. Significance of the alliance.
    c. Lesser Austrian alliances with Serbia and Rumania (1881, 1883).
    d. The Mediterranean agreements between England, Austria, and Italy (1887).

C. Bismarck's diplomacy at its zenith.
    1. Secures German colonies by playing off one power against another.
    2. Gradually isolates France and maintains status quo in Near East by trying to draw Austria, Italy, Russia, various Balkan states, Spain, and England into a system of alliances.
    3. The Reinsurance Treaty with Russia (1887).
        a. Bismarck's attempt to make Russia a close ally.

D. International relations after Bismarck's fall.
    1. William II, advised by Baron von Holstein, abandons Russia and protects Austria's position as a great power.
    2. Attempts to bring England into the Triple Alliance.
        a. England's policy of "splendid isolation."

E. Formation of the Dual Alliance between France and Russia (1893).
    1. Revival of the *revanche* movement in France (1885).
        a. Clemenceau becomes the leader.
    2. The Boulanger affair.
    3. Russia's growing fear of the Triple Alliance apparently supported by England.
    4. The Dual Alliance; a military convention (1893); significance,—the establishment of the balance of power in Europe.

F. Russia's troubles in the Far East.
1. England deserts China and supports Japan in order to check Russian advance.
2. Russo-Japanese War (1904–1905).
G. Remarkable expansion of German commerce.
1. German interests in Far East.
2. Bad blood between England and Germany.
   a. The Boer affair.
H. The formation of the Triple Entente (1904–1907).
1. England, France, and Russia settle their colonial rivalries.
2. General preparations for "Der Tag."
3. Italy and Spain arrange "friendly understandings" with France (1900, 1902, and 1904), and Japan, as an ally of England, is in the "sphere" of the Triple Entente.
4. The United States favors the Triple Entente.
   a. Roosevelt's interest in the Algeciras Conference (1906).
   b. The Root-Takahira agreement between the United States and Japan (1908).
5. The Triple Alliance starts to crack.
I. Germany's visions of being encircled by iron,—surrounded by enemies.
1. She increases her fleet regardless of England's opposition.
2. She tries to break the Triple Entente.
   a. In the Moroccan crises (1905–1906).
3. Attempts to make an agreement with Russia at Björkö (1905).
J. The Triple Entente continues to function.
1. Fear of the German and Austrian advance in Near East.
   a. Bagdad railway.
2. Russia, directed by Alexander Isvolski, develops a profound interest in the "Straits Question."
   a. Isvolski of Russia and Aehrenthal of Austria agree to support Austrian claims to Bosnia-Herzegovina, and Russia desires to have Straits agreements modified.

3. Austria, backed by Germany, obtains Bosnia-Herzegovina, but Isvolski does not succeed in his efforts to solve the Straits problem.
4. Rising suspicions and hatred between the Triple Alliance and the Triple Entente.
   a. The Moroccan affair (1911).
   b. The war between Italy and Turkey.
   c. Failure on the part of England and Germany to settle their rivalries.
5. The Balkan Wars almost start a general European catastrophe.
   a. From that time on Russia anticipates a European war.

K. The European situation on the eve of the World War.
1. Europe an armed camp.
2. England and Germany in desperate race for naval supremacy.
3. England, France, Germany, and Russia making military and naval preparations so as to be ready in case of war.
4. Importance of being the first one to "draw."

L. Causes of the war.
1. General causes: nationalism, imperialism, militarism. Mediate cause: the selfish, treacherous, and secret diplomacy behind the system of alliances.
2. The immediate cause of the war: the murder of the Archduke Francis Ferdinand.
   a. Diplomatic developments between 1912–1914.
      (1) The strengthening of the Franco-Russian alliance.
      (2) The growing hatred between Serbia and Austria.
   b. Isvolski and Poincaré "Balkanize" the Franco-Russian alliance, and Poincaré has visions of the day of *revanche*.
      (1) Russia given a free hand in Balkans by France.
      (2) Russia encourages Serbia in her opposition to Austria.

(3) England under Grey tacitly supports French and Russian ambitions as the lesser of two evils, the other evil being Germany.

c. The "upshot,"—the assassination of the Archduke Francis Ferdinand at Sarajevo (June 28, 1914).

(1) Significance of Poincaré's visit to St. Petersburg (July, 1914).

(2) Serbia's part in the murder of the archduke.

(3) Franco-Russian policy after the murder: "The war is inevitable."

(4) Austria's policy: punish Serbia or have an internal revolution.

(5) Germany's policy: a local affair in Austria's hands.

(6) The significance of Russia's mobilization of troops: a general European war inevitable.

(7) French encouragement of Russian aggression, and efforts to appear on the defensive.

(8) Germany's tardy attempts to prevent the war.

(9) Germany's responsibility for the conflict.

(10) Germany declares war on Russia because of Russia's general mobilization.

(11) England's part in bringing about the conflict.

(a) Grey's policy.

1) Refuses to change the Entente to an alliance; England therefore not duly bound to support France or Russia.

2) At the same time, through military and naval agreements, Grey indirectly encourages France and Russia in their plans to start a world war.

(12) German invasion of Belgium. (The assignment in Flick's *World History, 1776–1926*, in the collateral reading, might well be required.)

Principal Assignment

ROBINSON, *An Introduction to the History of Western Europe*, Vol. II, pp. 443–454.

Map Study

(World.) Trace the important territorial possessions of the leading powers involved in the World War, and note on the map the geographical elements which influenced the nations to enter the war.

Collateral Reading

FLICK, *Modern World History, 1776–1926*, pp. 503–554.

HAYES, *A Political and Social History of Modern Europe*, Vol. II, chap. xxx.

COOLIDGE, *The Origins of the Triple Alliance*, pp. 142–218.

GOOCH, *History of Modern Europe*, pp. 532–559.

DICKINSON, *The International Anarchy, 1904–1914*, pp. 399–478.

MONTGELAS, *The Case for the Central Powers*, pp. 11–112.

BARNES, *The Genesis of the World War*, pp. 1–90.

EWART, J. S., *The Roots and Causes of the Wars (1914–1918)*, Vol. I, pp. 451–491, German imperialism and German militarism.

DENNETT, *Roosevelt and the Russo-Japanese War*, selections.

SEYMOUR, *The Diplomatic Background of the World War*, selections.

XIV. THE WORLD WAR

A. Military events (1914–1915).
1. Invasion of Belgium.
2. Battle of the Marne.
3. The western front by the end of the winter.
4. Russian invasion of East Prussia.
   a. Tannenberg.
5. Russian invasion of Galicia.
   a. Surrender of Warsaw (August, 1915).
6. Enlistment of Turkey by the Central Powers (November, 1914).
   a. English invasion of Mesopotamia.

B. The conflict becomes a World War.
1. The fatal Dardanelles campaign (spring of 1915).
2. Italy joins the allied cause (May, 1915).
3. Nations engaged in war by summer of 1915.

C. The conflict on the sea.
1. The importance of the submarine.
2. England's use of the blockade.
3. The submarine, the blockade, and neutral rights.
4. Sinking of the *Lusitania* (May, 1915).
   a. Effect upon the world.

D. The rise of German fortunes.
1. The invasion of Serbia.
2. Bulgaria enters the war (October, 1915).
3. Conquest of Serbia.
   a. Supremacy of Central Powers in Near East.
4. Germans decide to end war by the capture of Verdun.
   a. The great drive (February–July, 1916).

b. The counter-attack on the Somme (July–November, 1916).

c. The Italian retreat before the Austrian drive (May, 1916).

d. A successful Russian offensive brings Rumania into the war (1916).

e. The invasion and conquest of Rumania by the Central Powers.

(1) Capture of Bucharest (December, 1916).

f. Aërial warfare; its importance in the World War.

E. The intervention of the United States (1917).

1. Difficulties confronting the United States in her efforts to remain neutral during the war.

a. Allied and German propaganda.

b. Sympathy of various nationalities in the United States for "the old country."

c. Economic interests of the United States.

(1) Trade.

(2) Loans.

(3) Blockades.

2. The submarine controversy.

a. President Wilson's opposition to "unrestricted use" of the submarine.

b. The German "peace drive" (December, 1916).

c. Great Britain's extension of the blockade forces Germany to revert to the "unrestricted use" of submarines.

d. The United States breaks off diplomatic relations with Germany (February 3, 1917).

3. War between the United States and Germany is declared (April 6, 1917).

a. Significance.

(1) Resources of the United States in war,—money and materials.

(2) Other nations follow the United States into war.

(3) The conflict involves, directly or indirectly, every country and individual in the world.

F. The Russian Revolution of 1917 and its influence upon the course of the war.

  1. Causes.

    a. Corruption and inefficiency of the autocratic government.

    b. Bread riots.

  2. The political revolution.

    a. The new provisional government (March 15, 1917).

    b. The formation of the revolutionary cabinet.

      (1) Alexander Kerensky.

      (2) Proposed reforms.

      (3) Attempts to continue the war.

  3. The economic revolution (November, 1917).

    a. The "soviet" in Petrograd.

    b. The dictatorship of the proletariat.

      (1) Lenin and Trotzky, leaders of the Bolsheviki.

    c. The administration of the Bolsheviki.

      (1) Attempts to institute a "communist system."

      (2) Peace negotiations with Central Powers (December, 1917).

        (*a*) Treaty of Brest-Litovsk (March 3, 1918); its importance.

G. The Allied victory (1917–1918).

  1. Chief military events of 1917; Germans return to "Hindenburg" line.

  2. The capture of Bagdad and Jerusalem.

  3. Great German drives on western front (March–July, 1918).

    a. Failure of submarine campaign.

    b. Russian Revolution enables Germans to concentrate on western front.

    c. The attempt to capture Amiens.

    d. Appointment of General Foch as commander-in-chief of western front.

    e. German drive between Arras and Ypres.

    f. Drive on Château-Thierry.

      (1) Americans help check Germans.

    g. Achievements of America in the war.

      (1) Capture of St. Mihiel.

      (2) The Argonne Forest and the capture of Sedan (November 7, 1918).

H. Collapse of the Central Powers.

  1. Opposition to Germany.

    a. On the eastern front.

    b. In the Balkans; Bulgaria surrenders (September 29, 1918).

    c. Turkey accepts terms of surrender (October 31, 1918).

  2. Failure of Germans to starve England.

  3. The well-nigh inexhaustible resources of the United States.

    a. Failure of the submarine campaign.

  4. Unconditional surrender of Austria-Hungary (November 3, 1918).

  5. The fall of the German Empire and the signing of the Armistice (November 11, 1918).

    a. Its terms.

I. Costs of the World War in life and treasure.

Principal Assignment

    ROBINSON, *An Introduction to the History of Western Europe,* Vol. II, pp. 454–476.

Map Study

    (Europe and the world.) Locate the places where the principal battles occurred on land and sea. Also sketch the trench lines on the various fronts and note the important changes during the course of the war.

Collateral Reading

HAYES, *A Political and Social History of Modern Europe*, Vol. II, chaps. xxxi, xxxiv.

TURNER, *Europe since 1789*, chap. xxiii.

FUETER, *World History, 1815–1920*, pp. 423–473.

GOOCH, *History of Modern Europe*, pp. 560–658.

GIBBONS, *Introduction to World Politics*, pp. 272–304, 318–327.

JOHNSON, *Topography and Strategy in the War*, pp. 1–49.

HAYES, *A Brief History of the World War*, pp. 143–200.

POLLARD, *A Short History of the Great War*, selections.

XV. READJUSTMENT AND RECONSTRUCTION AFTER THE WORLD WAR

A. The Treaty of Versailles.
  1. Those responsible for it.
     a. The representatives of the five great powers organize the conference.
     b. The delegates of other powers are present.
     c. The "Big Three" render the important decisions.
  2. The Treaty.
     a. Territorial settlements; other terms; the *reparations* problem; German attitude toward the Treaty.
B. Founding of the League of Nations.
  1. Its importance.
  2. Its organization.
  3. Its powers; Article X.
  4. The Court of International Justice (World Court).
  5. The International Labor Organization.
C. Opposition in the United States to joining the League of Nations.
  1. "Entangling alliances."
  2. Objections to Article X.
D. The United States refuses to enter the League and signs a separate peace with Germany (July 2, 1921).
E. The new map of Europe.
  1. The German Republic.
  2. Dissolution of Austria-Hungary.
     a. Creation of the republic of Czechoslovakia and the kingdom of Jugoslavia.
     b. The last of the Hapsburgs.
     c. Austria after the war.

d. Hungary after the war.

e. The republic of Czechoslovakia.

f. The kingdom of Jugoslavia.

3. The restoration of Poland.

4. Trotzky and his "Red Army" enable the Bolsheviki to retain control of Russia.

5. The new nations around the Baltic.

   a. Finland, Esthonia, Latvia, and Lithuania.

6. The Balkans after the war.

   a. Bulgaria and Rumania.

   b. Turkey.

      (1) Treaties of Sèvres (1920) and Lausanne (1923).

      (2) Kemal Pasha and the new Turkish Republic (1923).

F. The aftermath of the war.

   1. The chief ambition of the diplomats at the Congress of Vienna (1815): restore the old régime; "legitimacy."

   2. Principal political ambitions of the diplomats at Versailles.

      a. Abolition of autocracy.

      b. Right of nations to self-determination.

   3. Political results of the war.

      a. Fall of the Hohenzollerns, Hapsburgs, Romanovs, and Ottoman Empire.

      b. The new republics.

   4. The question of reparations.

      a. Attempt to make Germany pay for the war.

      b. The so-called Dawes plan.

   5. The question of disarmament.

      a. The conference at Washington (1921).

      b. President Coolidge tries to call another conference (1927).

   6. Attempts of League of Nations to solve world problems.

      a. Political problems.

      b. Financial troubles.

      c. Humanitarian activities of the League.

7. The World Court.
   a. Organization and duties.
   b. The old Court of Arbitration.
   c. The United States and the World Court.
8. Pacts and plans to end wars.
   a. The Draft Treaty of Mutual Assistance (1924).
   b. The "American plan" (1924).
   c. The Geneva Protocol (1924).
   d. The Locarno treaties (1925).
      (1) Importance; a federation of states of Europe.
      (2) Germany enters the League of Nations and Spain withdraws (1926).
      (3) The Council of the League is "enlarged."

Principal Assignment

ROBINSON, *An Introduction to the History of Western Europe*, Vol. II, pp. 477–504.

Map Study

(Europe.) Note the territorial changes in Europe which have resulted from the World War.

Collateral Reading

HAYES, *A Political and Social History of Modern Europe*, Vol. II, chap. xxxii.

GIBBONS. *Europe since 1918*, pp. 18–93, 346–367, 491–504, 544–598.

VIALLATE, *Economic Imperialism*, pp. 127–170.

FLICK, *Modern World History, 1776–1926*, pp. 573–659.

GOOCH, *History of Modern Europe*, pp. 659–696.

GOOCH, *Germany*, pp. 190–209, 232–275.

MOON, *Imperialism and World Politics*, pp. 473–566.

HARRIS, *Europe and the East*, pp. 577–620.

EARLE, *Turkey, the Great Powers, and the Bagdad Railway*, pp. 275–306.

BOWMAN, *The New World, Problems in Political Geography*, selections.

Also consult the *Current History* magazine or some other reliable periodical for the years 1918 to the present time, and read substantial articles concerning problems of reconstruction after the war.

XVI. THE DEVELOPMENT OF HUMAN KNOWLEDGE

A. The fundamental rôle of knowledge in human affairs.
  1. Our civilization the result of the expansion of human knowledge.
    a. By discoveries and inventions.
  2. The expansion will continue.
B. The world in which man lives and his general position in the whole order of nature.
  1. The great age of the earth.
    a. Origin of the earth.
    b. Its relation to the universe.
    c. Geological contributions to the study of the origin of the earth.
  2. The theory of evolution.
    a. Buffon's, Lamarck's, and Herbert Spencer's concepts of evolution.
    b. Charles Darwin's *Origin of Species by Means of Natural Selection.*
    c. "The struggle for existence."
      (1) Alfred R. Wallace and the doctrine of *variation* and the *survival of the fittest.*
  3. Opposition to the theory of evolution.
    a. Religious opposition.
    b. The attempt to create an issue between science and religion.
    c. The growing conviction that science and religion have definite spheres and should coöperate rather than oppose each other.

4. The remarkable development of science.
   a. The study of living cells and its results.
     (1) The compound microscope.
     (2) Observations of Schleiden, Schwann, and Von Mohl.
        (a) *Cells* and *protoplasm.*
   b. Importance of the microscopic study of cells.
   c. Embryology,—the science of germ cells.
     (1) Influence of *heredity* and *environment* on life and its development.
   d. Bacteria and the germ theory of disease.
     (1) Early discovery of bacteria.
     (2) Contributions of Pasteur, Koch, and Jenner.
C. Development of surgery.
   1. Use of anæsthetics; use of antiseptics; Lister.
   2. Pasteur and treatment of hydrophobia.
   3. Metchnikov and the white blood corpuscles.
D. The study of *inert* matter.
   1. The atom.
     a. Importance of X rays and radium.
     b. Attempts to break up the atom.
       (1) *Nucleus* and *electrons.*
       (2) Failure to change constitution of atom.
     c. *Molecules:* clusters of atoms.
     d. What scientists achieve by juggling the atoms about.
   2. The importance of modern chemistry.
     a. Biochemistry,—the chemistry of life.
E. Modern ways of studying man himself,—his nature, achievements, and possibilities.
   1. Scientific method as used in the study of natural science.
     a. No place in science for dogma.
     b. The *genetic* method.
     c. The comparative method.
     d. Experimentation and "control."
   2. Man an important but difficult subject of scientific study.

F. The newer aims of historical study.

   1. The new *genetic*, or developmental, method of historical study.

   2. The study of the history of history.

   3. The increase in the scope of history.

G. The perspective of human development.

   1. Difficult questions of the origin and development of man.

     a. The story of his fall from a state of perfection, or of his rise.

   2. The comparative study of mankind and its fruits.

     a. Recent development of the study of primitive culture.

       (1) Anthropology; its importance.

         (*a*) Enables us to determine the origin and development of many existing customs and to criticize many practices of our own which we commonly take for granted.

     b. The results of the comparative study of mankind.

       (1) The *mores*, or customs.

       (2) Animism and taboo among primitive and modern peoples.

       (3) Race prejudice and nationalism weakened as a result of anthropological research.

   3. The new methods of studying the mind.

     a. Application of comparative and genetic methods in the study of individual mental developments.

       (1) Psychology; its aim "to cast light on man's still mysterious ways of feeling and acting and on his responses and adjustments to his surroundings."

       (2) Ideas of the soul.

       (3) Study of behavior from childhood on; importance of early impressions; the unconscious.

       (4) Abnormal psychology.

   4. The problems of education.

     a. Factors in the education of an individual.

    b. The history of education.

    c. Difficulties confronting educational reformers in their attempts to guide the four fifths of education that the average individual receives outside the school.

    d. Importance of liberty in the matter of teaching and in the expression of ideas.

  5. The "new" history.

H. Plans for bettering human relations.

  1. The vast increase of human knowledge has tended to augment beyond belief the *possibilities* of life.

  2. The phrase "Liberty, Equality, and Fraternity" as an expression of historical achievements.

  3. The significance of the word "democracy."

  4. The "reformers" in history.

  5. The importance of economic and social reforms in the nineteenth and twentieth centuries.

    a. Beginning of socialism.

      (1) The utopians.

  6. Marx and the theory of the class struggle.

    a. The *Communist Manifesto.*

    b. *Das Kapital.*

    c. Marx's materialistic interpretation of history; the *class war* inevitable.

    d. Spread of his ideas.

    e. The formation of the "International."

  7. The standard arguments against socialism.

  8. The Russian experiment in communism.

    a. Lenin's attempt to carry out a complete social and economic revolution.

    b. The All-Russian Congress of Soviets (July, 1918) establishes a constitution.

    c. Nature of the Socialist Soviet Republic.

  9. Important changes adopted in the new constitution of the Russian Socialist Soviet Republic.

10. Spread of communism in Germany, Hungary, and Italy.
11. Opposition to spread of communism.
    a. Opposition to the moderate socialists in Germany.
    b. Admiral Horthy, the reactionary leader in Hungary.
    c. Mussolini and the party called the *Fascisti* in Italy.
12. The rise of the British Labor party.
    a. Its origin.
    b. Its labor ministry of 1923.
       (1) Ramsay MacDonald's administration.
    c. Return of conservative party to power.
       (1) Stanley Baldwin and the great strike in 1926.
13. The importance of science in the solution of social and economic problems.
14. The future in the light of the present and the past.

Principal Assignment

ROBINSON, *An Introduction to the History of Western Europe*, Vol. II, pp. 505–586.

Collateral Reading

ROBINSON and BEARD, *Readings*, Vol. II, pp. 467–519.

Rapid Collateral Reading.

The student should read during the semester a minimum of 250 pages from one or more of the books listed below and should be prepared to give an individual report either in personal conference or in writing.

BAIN, *The First Romanovs.*
REDDAWAY, *Frederick the Great.*
YOUNG, *The Life of Frederick the Great.*
BRIGHT, *Maria Theresa.*
BRIGHT, *Joseph II.*
LOWELL, *The Eve of the French Revolution.*
BELLOC, *Marie Antoinette.*
BELLOC, *High Lights of the French Revolution* (also entitled, *The Last Days of the French Monarchy*).
BEESLY, *Life of Danton.*

FISHER, *Napoleon.*

JOHNSTON, *Napoleon.*

TARBELL, *A Life of Napoleon Bonaparte, with a Sketch of Josephine.*

FREKSA, *A Peace Congress of Intrigue.*

TREVELYAN, *Garibaldi and the Making of Italy.*

MARTINENGO-CESARESCO, *Cavour.*

GUEDALLA, *The Second Empire.*

SMITH, *Bismarck.*

DESCHANEL, *Gambetta.*

MOON, *Imperialism and World Politics.*

GILES, *The Civilization of China.*

LATOURETTE, *The Development of Japan.*

KORFF, *Russia's Foreign Relations during the Last Half-Century.*

COOLIDGE, *The Origins of the Triple Alliance.*

HYNDMAN, *Clemenceau, the Man and his Time.*

DENNETT, *Roosevelt and the Russo-Japanese War.*

DICKINSON, *The International Anarchy.*

HAYES, *A Brief History of the World War.*

TOYNBEE and KIRKWOOD, *Turkey.*

TOYNBEE, *The Western Question in Greece and Turkey.*

SEYMOUR, *Woodrow Wilson and the World War.*

BEARD, *Cross Currents in Europe Today.*

GOOCH, *Germany.*

CHIROL, *The Occident and the Orient.*

HARRIS, *Europe and the East.*

SEDGWICK and TYLER, *A Short History of Science.*

HOLMES, *Pasteur.*

MUMFORD, *The Story of Utopias.*

APPENDIX A

OPTIONAL AND COLLATERAL READING

The readings suggested in the syllabus are grouped under three divisions: first, the principal, or required, readings; second, the collateral readings; and, third, the rapid collateral readings. The student might well purchase the books referred to in the principal assignments; for the collateral readings a number of copies of each work referred to should be provided by the library.

ADAMS, G. B., *An Outline Sketch of English Constitutional History*. New Haven, 1918.

ADAMS, G. B., *Civilization during the Middle Ages*. New York, 1894.

ADAMS, G. B., *The Growth of the French Nation*. New York, 1896.

ALLEN, P. S., *The Age of Erasmus*. Oxford, 1914.

ANDREWS, C. M., *The Historical Development of Modern Europe* (two volumes in one). New York, 1900.

ARMSTRONG, E., *Lorenzo de' Medici and Florence in the Fifteenth Century*. New York, 1896.

BAIN, R. N., *The First Romanovs (1613–1725)*. London, 1905.

BARNES, H. E., *The Genesis of the World War*. New York, 1926.

BASSETT, J. S., *A Short History of the United States, 1492–1920*. New York, 1921.

BEARD, C. A. *Cross Currents in Europe Today*. New York, 1922.

BEAZLEY, C. R., FORBES, N., and BIRKETT, G. A., *Russia from the Varangians to the Bolsheviks*. Oxford, 1918.

BEESLY, A. H., *Life of Danton*. London, 1899.

BEESLY, E. S., *Queen Elizabeth*. New York, 1892.

BELLOC, H., *High Lights of the French Revolution* (also entitled *The Last Days of the French Monarchy*). New York, 1915.

BELLOC, H., *Marie Antoinette*. New York, 1909.

BOLTON, H. E., *The Spanish Borderlands*. New Haven, 1921.

BOLTON, H. E., and MARSHALL, T. M., *The Colonization of North America, 1492–1783*. New York, 1920.

BOTSFORD, G. W., and BOTSFORD, L. S., *A Source Book of Ancient History*. New York, 1913.

BOURNE, H. E., *The Revolutionary Period in Europe (1763-1815)*. New York, 1917.

BOURRIENNE, L. A. F., *Memoirs of Napoleon Bonaparte*, edited by R. W. Phipps (2 vols.). New York, 1885.

BOWMAN, I., *The New World—Problems in Political Geography*. New York, 1922.

BREASTED, J. H., *Ancient Times, a History of the Early World*. New York, 1916.

BRIDGES, J. H., *France under Richelieu and Colbert*. London, 1912.

BRIGHT, J. F., *Joseph II*. London, 1897.

BRIGHT, J. F., *Maria Theresa*. London, 1897.

Cambridge Modern History, edited by Lord Acton (14 vols.). Cambridge, England, 1902-1912.

CARLYLE, T., *Frederick the Great*, edited by A. M. D. Hughes. Oxford, 1916.

CARLYLE, T., *The French Revolution* (3 vols.). London, 1902.

CHAPMAN, C. E., *A History of Spain*. New York, 1918.

CHEYNEY, E. P., *A Short History of England*. Boston, 1919.

CHEYNEY, E. P., *European Background of American History, 1300-1600* (American Nation Series). New York, 1904.

CHIROL, V., *The Occident and the Orient*. Chicago, 1924.

COOLIDGE, A. C., *The Origins of the Triple Alliance*. New York, 1917.

DAVIS, H. W. C., *Charlemagne (Charles the Great) the Hero of Two Nations*. New York, 1900.

DAVIS, W. S., *Life on a Medieval Barony; a Picture of a Typical Feudal Community in the Thirteenth Century*. New York, 1901.

DAVIS, W. S., *The Influence of Wealth in Imperial Rome*. New York, 1910.

DAWSON, W. H., *The Evolution of Modern Germany*. New York, 1919.

DAY, C. A., *A History of Commerce*. New York, 1914.

DENNETT, T., *Roosevelt and the Russo-Japanese War*. New York, 1925.

DESCHANEL, P. E. L., *Gambetta*. London, 1920.

DICKINSON, G. L., *The International Anarchy, 1904-1914*. New York, 1926.

DILL, S., *Roman Society in the Last Century of the Western Empire*. New York, 1899.

DOUGLAS, R. K., *Europe and the Far East, 1506-1912*. New York, 1913.

DUNN PATTISON, R. P., *Leading Figures in European History*. New York, 1912.

EARLE, E. M., *Turkey, the Great Powers, and the Bagdad Railway; A Study in Imperialism*. New York, 1923.

EMERTON, E., *An Introduction to the Study of the Middle Ages (375-814)*. Boston, 1888.

EMERTON, E., *Medieval Europe (814-1300)*. Boston, 1894.

EMERTON, E., *The Beginnings of Modern Europe (1250-1450)*. Boston, 1917.

EWART, J. S., *The Roots and Causes of the Wars (1914–1918)* (2 vols.). New York, 1925.

FARMER, J. E., *Versailles and the Court under Louis XIV.* New York, 1906.

FISHER, H. A. L., *Napoleon* (Home University Library). New York, 1913.

FLICK, A. C., *Modern World History, 1776–1926.* New York, 1926.

FLING, F. M., and FLING, H. D., *Source Problems on the French Revolution.* New York, 1913.

FOURNIER, A., *Napoleon the First*, edited by E. G. Bourne. New York, 1903.

FREKSA, F., *A Peace Congress of Intrigue (Vienna, 1815)*, translated by H. Hansen. New York, 1919.

FUETER, E., *World History, 1815–1920*, translated by S. B. Fay. New York, 1922.

GIBBINS, H. de B., *The Industrial History of England.* London, 1919.

GIBBON, E., *The Decline and Fall of the Roman Empire* (Everyman's Library; 6 vols.). New York, 1910.

GIBBONS, H. A., *An Introduction to World Politics.* New York, 1922.

GIBBONS, H. A., *Europe since 1918.* New York, 1923.

GIBBONS, H. A., *The New Map of Europe (1911–1914).* New York, 1914.

GILES, H. A., *The Civilization of China* (Home University Library). New York, 1911.

GOOCH, G. P., *Germany.* London, 1925.

GOOCH, G. P., *History of Modern Europe, 1878–1919.* New York, 1923.

GRANT, A. J., *The French Monarchy (1483–1789)* (2 vols.). Cambridge, 1914.

GREEN, J. R., *A Short History of the English People.* New York, 1890.

GUEDALLA, P., *The Second Empire.* New York, 1923.

GUÉRARD, A. L., *French Civilization in the Nineteenth Century.* New York, 1918.

HANOTAUX, G., *Contemporary France*, translated by J. C. Tarver (4 vols.). New York, 1903–1909.

HARRIS, N. D., *Europe and the East.* New York, 1926.

HASKINS, C. H., *The Normans in European History.* London, 1919.

HASKINS, C. H., *The Rise of Universities.* New York, 1923.

HASKINS, C. H., and LORD, R. H., *Some Problems of the Peace Conference.* Cambridge, 1920.

HASSALL, A., *Louis XIV and the Zenith of the French Monarchy.* New York, 1902.

HAYES, C. J. H., *A Brief History of the Great War.* New York, 1920.

HAYES, C. J. H., *A Political and Social History of Modern Europe* (2 vols.). New York, 1924.

HAYES, C. J. H., *Essays on Nationalism.* New York, 1926.

HAZEN, C. D., *Europe since 1815* (2 vols.). New York, 1923.

HAZEN, C. D., *Modern Europe*. New York, 1924.

HEADLAM, J. W., *Bismarck and the Foundation of the German Empire*. New York, 1899.

HENDERSON, E. F., *A Short History of Germany* (2 vols.). New York, 1916.

HOBSON, J. A., *Imperialism, a Study*. London, 1902.

HOLMES, S. J., *Pasteur*. New York, 1924.

HOWE, F. C., *Socialized Germany*. New York, 1915.

HUGON, C., *Social France in the XVII Century*. New York, 1911.

HUME, M. A. S., *Philip II of Spain*. London, 1917.

HYNDMAN, H. M., *Clemenceau, the Man and his Time*. New York, 1919.

JACKSON, S. M., *Huldreich Zwingli*. New York, 1903.

JACOBS, H. E., *Martin Luther, the Hero of the Reformation, 1483–1546*. New York, 1909.

JESSOPP, A., *The Coming of the Friars, and other Historical Essays*. New York, 1913.

JOHNSON, A. H., *Europe in the Sixteenth Century*. London, 1909.

JOHNSON, D. W., *Topography and Strategy in the War*. New York, 1917.

JOHNSTON, R. M., *Napoleon*. New York, 1904.

JOHNSTON, R. M., *The French Revolution*. New York, 1909.

KNIGHT, M. M., *Economic History of Europe to the End of the Middle Ages*. New York, 1926.

KORFF, S. A., *Russia's Foreign Relations during the Last Half-Century*. New York, 1922.

LANE-POOLE, S., *Saladin; and the Fall of the Kingdom of Jerusalem*. New York, 1903.

LANE-POOLE, S., *The Speeches and Table-Talk of the Prophet Mohammed*. New York, 1905.

LANE-POOLE, S., *The Story of the Moors in Spain*. New York, 1903.

LANE-POOLE, S., *The Story of Turkey*. New York, 1897.

LATOURETTE, K. S., *The Development of Japan*. New York, 1918.

LAVISSE, E., *The Youth of Frederick the Great*, translated by M. B. Coleman. Chicago, 1892.

LOWELL, E. J., *The Eve of the French Revolution*. New York, 1892.

LUCHAIRE, A., *Social France at the Time of Philip Augustus*, translated by E. B. Krehbiel. New York, 1912.

LYBYER, A. H., *The Government of the Ottoman Empire in the Time of Suleiman the Magnificent*. Cambridge, 1913.

MACAULAY, T. B. (Lord), *Critical and Historical Essays* (2 vols.). New York, 1910–1913.

McCABE, J., *Peter Abélard*. New York, 1901.

MADELIN, L., *The French Revolution*. London, 1922.

MAHAFFY, J. P., *Social Life in Greece from Homer to Menander*. London, 1894.

MAHAN, A. T., *The Influence of Sea Power upon the French Revolution and Empire, 1793–1812* (2 vols.). New York, 1910.

MARRIOTT, J. A. R., and ROBERTSON, C. G., *The Evolution of Prussia*. Oxford, 1917.

MARTINENGO-CESARESCO, E., *Cavour*. London, 1921.

MATHEWS, S., *The French Revolution, 1789–1815*. London, 1923.

MILLER, W., *The Balkans*. New York, 1911.

MILYOUKOV, P. N., *Russia and its Crisis*. Chicago, 1905.

MONTGELAS, M., *The Case for the Central Powers*, translated by C. Vesey. New York, 1925.

MOON, P. T., *Imperialism and World Politics*. New York, 1926.

MORFILL, W. R., *Poland*. New York, 1893.

MORFILL, W. R., *Russia*. New York, 1901.

MORLEY, J., *Critical Miscellanies* (3 vols.). London, 1888.

MORLEY, J., *Oliver Cromwell*. London, 1900.

MORRIS, W. A., *The Early English County Court* (University of California Publications in History, Vol. XIV, No. 2, pp. 89–230). Berkeley, 1926.

MORRIS, W. A., *The Medieval English Sheriff*. London, 1927.

MUMFORD, L., *The Story of Utopias*. New York, 1922.

MUNRO, D. C., *The Middle Ages, 395–1272*. New York, 1921.

MUNRO, D. C., and SELLERY, G. C., *Medieval Civilization*. New York, 1910.

MUNRO, W. B., *Crusaders of New France*. New Haven, 1918.

OGG, F. A., *A Source Book of Medieval History*. New York, 1908.

OGG, F. A., *Economic Development of Modern Europe*. New York, 1920.

OGG, F. A., *Social Progress in Contemporary Europe*. New York, 1912.

PALM, F. C.. *Politics and Religion in Sixteenth-Century France*. Boston, 1927.

PARES, B., *A History of Russia*. New York, 1926.

PARKMAN, F., *Montcalm and Wolfe* (2 vols.). Boston, 1910.

PATER, W. H., *The Renaissance; Studies in Art and Poetry*. New York, 1903.

PERKINS, J. B., *France under Louis XV* (2 vols.). New York, 1897.

PERKINS, J. B., *Richelieu and the Growth of French Power*. New York, 1900.

POLLARD, A. F., *A Short History of the Great War*. New York, 1920.

PRIEST, G. M., *Germany since 1740*. New York, 1914.

PRIESTLEY, H. I., *The Mexican Nation, a History*. New York, 1923.

PUTNAM, R., *William the Silent, Prince of Orange* (2 vols.). New York, 1898.

REDDAWAY, W. F., *Frederick the Great and the Rise of Prussia*. New York, 1911.

REINACH, S., *Apollo*. London, 1917.

RICHMAN, I. B., *The Spanish Conquerors*. New Haven, 1921.

ROBINSON, H., *The Development of the British Empire*. New York, 1922.

ROBINSON, J. H., *Readings in European History* (2 vols.). Boston, 1904.

ROBINSON, J. H., and BEARD, C. A., *Readings in Modern European History* (2 vols.). Boston, 1909.

ROBINSON, J. H., and ROLFE, H. W., *Petrarch, the First Modern Scholar and Man of Letters*. Boston, 1899.

ROBINSON, J. H., SMITH, E. P., and BREASTED, J. H., *Our World Today and Yesterday*. Boston, 1924.

ROSE, J. H., *Nationality in Modern History*. New York, 1916.

ROSE, J. H., *The Development of the European Nations, 1870–1921*. (Two volumes in one.) New York, 1922.

ROSE, J. H., *The Life of Napoleon I* (2 vols.). New York, 1902.

SABATIER, P., *Life of St. Francis of Assisi*. New York, 1912.

SAYCE, A. H., *Babylonians and Assyrians, Life and Customs*. New York, 1914.

SCHAPIRO, J. S., *Modern and Contemporary European History*. New York, 1921.

SCHAPIRO, J. S., *Social Reform and the Reformation*. New York, 1909.

SCHEVILL, F., *A History of Europe from the Reformation to our Own Day*. New York, 1925.

SCHURMAN, J. G., *The Balkan Wars, 1912–1913*. Princeton, 1914.

SEDGWICK, W. T., and TYLER, H. W., *A Short History of Science*. New York, 1917.

SÉE, H., *Economic and Social Conditions in France during the Eighteenth Century*, translated by E. H. Zeydel. New York, 1927.

SEEBOHM, F., *The Era of the Protestant Revolution*. New York, 1912.

SEELEY, J. R., *The Expansion of England*. London, 1883.

SEIGNOBOS, C., *The Feudal Régime*, translated by E. W. Dow. New York, 1890.

SEYMOUR, C., *The Diplomatic Background of the War, 1870–1914*. New Haven, 1916.

SEYMOUR, C., *Woodrow Wilson and the World War, a Chronicle of our Own Times*. New Haven, 1921.

SICHEL, E. H., *The Renaissance* (Home University Library). New York, 1914.

SKRINE, F. H., *The Expansion of Russia*. Cambridge, 1915.

SMITH, M., *Bismarck and German Unity*. New York, 1923.

SMITH, P., *Conversations with Luther*. New York, 1915.

SMITH, P., *Erasmus; a Study of his Life, Ideals, and Place in History*. New York, 1923.

SMITH, P., *The Age of the Reformation*. New York, 1920.

STEPHENS, H. M., *A History of the French Revolution* (2 vols.). New York, 1886–1902.

SYMONDS, J. A., *A Short History of the Renaissance in Italy*, edited by A. Pearson. New York, 1894.

TARBELL, I. M., *A Life of Napoleon Bonaparte; with a Sketch of Josephine, Empress of the French*. New York, 1918.

THAYER, W. R., *Throne-Makers*. Boston, 1899.

THORNDIKE, L., *The History of Medieval Europe*. New York, 1917.

TOYNBEE, A. J., *The Western Question in Greece and Turkey*. London, 1922.

TOYNBEE, A. J., and KIRKWOOD, K. P., *Turkey*. New York, 1927.

TREVELYAN, G. M., *England under the Stuarts*. New York, 1904.

TREVELYAN, G. M., *Garibaldi and the Making of Italy*. New York, 1911.

TURNER, E. R. *Europe since 1789*. New York, 1920.

VAN DYKE, P., *Ignatius Loyola*. New York, 1926.

VEDDER, H. C., *The Reformation in Germany*. New York, 1914.

VIALLATE, A., *Economic Imperialism and International Relations during the Last Fifty Years*. New York, 1923.

VOLTAIRE, F. M. A., *Age of Louis XIV*, translated by R. Griffith (3 vols.). London, 1779–1781.

WAKEMAN, H. O., *Europe, 1598–1715*. New York, 1916.

WALKER, W., *Great Men of the Christian Church*. Chicago, 1908.

WALLACE, D. M., *Russia*. New York, 1912.

WHITCOMB, M., *A Literary Source-Book of the Renaissance*. Philadelphia, 1903.

WHITE, A. D., *Seven Great Statesmen*. New York, 1910.

WOOD, W. C. H., *Elizabethan Sea-Dogs*. New Haven, 1920.

WOOLF, L. S., *Economic Imperialism*. New York, 1920.

WRIGHT, C. H. C., *The Background of Modern French Literature*. Boston, 1926.

YOUNG, A., *Travels in France by Arthur Young during the Years 1787, 1788, and 1789*, edited by M. Betham-Edwards. London, 1912.

YOUNG, N., *The Life of Frederick the Great*. New York, 1919.

APPENDIX B

HISTORICAL NOVELS

Historical novels have their place in the study of history. They add interest to the work and give local color and atmosphere to historical episodes. Material of this kind, however, must be used with care and discrimination.

The novels listed below might be assigned as a part of the collateral reading, although they are not so used in the course in European history as given in the University of California. Additional interest might be stimulated by having the student investigate the historical accuracy of the novel he selects.

AUTHOR	TITLE	SUBJECT
DAVIS, W. S.	Belshazzar	Fall of Babylon (538 B.C.)
DAVIS, W. S.	A Victor of Salamis	Greece (480–478 B.C.)
DAVIS, W. S.	A Friend of Cæsar	Roman .Republic (50–47 B.C.)
DAVIS, W. S.	The Beauty of the Purple	Constantinople in the eighth century
JAMES, G. P. R.	Philip Augustus	Medieval France
BULWER-LYTTON, E. G. E.	Rienzi, the Last of the Roman Tribunes	Medieval Rome
DAVIS, W. S.	"God Wills It!"	Crusades
SCOTT, SIR WALTER	The Talisman	Crusades
JAMES, G. P. R.	Agincourt	Hundred Years' War
JAMES, G. P. R.	The Jacquerie	Hundred Years' War
ELIOT, GEORGE	Romola	Savonarola
READE, CHARLES	The Cloister and the Hearth	Renaissance
CHARLES, MRS. ELIZABETH	Chronicles of the Schönberg-Cotta Family	Reformation
EBERS, GEORG	Barbara Blomberg	Charles V and Luther
HAUFF, WILHELM	Lichtenstein	The Peasants' Revolt

WEYMAN, S. J.	A Gentleman of France	French religious wars
DUMAS, ALEXANDRE	Marguerite of Valois	St. Bartholomew's Day
CRAWFORD, F. M.	In the Palace of the King	Spain under Philip II
TOLSTOĬ, A. K.	The Terrible Czar	Russia; Ivan IV
KINGSLEY, CHARLES	Westward Ho!	Elizabeth; Armada
JAMES, G. P. R.	One in a Thousand	Henry IV
RUNKLE, BERTHA	The Helmet of Navarre	Henry IV
SABATINI, RAFAEL	The Sea-Hawk	James I of England
DUMAS, ALEXANDRE	The Three Musketeers	Richelieu
JAMES, G. P. R.	Richelieu	Richelieu
WEYMAN, S. J.	Under the Red Robe	Richelieu
GRIMMELSHAUSEN, H. J. C., von	The Adventurous Simplicissimus	Thirty Years' War
WEYMAN, S. J.	My Lady Rotha	Thirty Years' War
DUMAS, ALEXANDRE	Twenty Years After	France; Mazarin
SIENKIEWICZ, HENRYK	With Fire and Sword ⎫	Poland and Russia in
SIENKIEWICZ, HENRYK	The Deluge ⎬	the middle of the
SIENKIEWICZ, HENRYK	Pan Michael ⎭	seventeenth century
SHORTHOUSE, J. H.	John Inglesant	Spain, Charles II
DOYLE, SIR ARTHUR CONAN	The Refugees	Louis XIV
DUMAS, ALEXANDRE	The Vicomte de Bragelonne	Louis XIV
SAND, GEORGE	Consuelo	Frederick the Great
SAND, GEORGE	The Countess of Rudolstadt	Frederick the Great
DUMAS, ALEXANDRE	The Queen's Necklace	The French Court in the eighteenth century
CHAMBERS, R. W.	The Red Republic	The Commune of Paris
CONRAD, JOSEPH	The Rover	French Revolution
DICKENS, CHARLES	A Tale of Two Cities	French Revolution
HUGO, V. M.	Ninety-Three	French Revolution
KIPLING, RUDYARD	"Brother Squaretoes," and "A Priest in Spite of Himself," in "Rewards and Fairies"	Revolutionary era
LEVER, C. J.	Tom Burke of "Ours"	French Revolution
SABATINI, RAFAEL	Scaramouche	French Revolution
WEYMAN, S. J.	The Red Cockade	French Revolution
DUMAS, ALEXANDRE	The Whites and the Blues	Rise of Napoleon

Tolstoï, Leo	War and Peace	Napoleon's invasion of Russia (counts as two novels)
Conrad, Joseph	Suspense	Napoleonic period
Hugo, V. M.	Les Misérables	France, 1815 (counts as two novels)
Meredith, George	Vittoria (and series)	Italian liberation, 1859
Merriman, H. S.	Flotsam	Indian mutiny
Zola, Émile	The Downfall	Franco-German War; Sedan
Chambers, R. W.	Lorraine	Franco-German War
Turgenev, Ivan	Fathers and Sons	Nihilism
Blasco Ibañez, Vincente	The Four Horsemen of the Apocalypse	World War
Empey, A. G.	"Over the Top"	World War
Wells, H. G.	Mr. Britling sees it Through	World War
Fogazzaro, Antonio	The Saint	Modernism
Suttner, B. von	Lay Down your Arms	Pacificism